"Several years ago I had the pleasure of discussing Ephesians with Chris Wright at his kitchen table. We sat with Bibles open, notes strewn everywhere, and a pot of tea. Chris's love for God, his scholarly expertise, and easy manner made for a delightful and enriching afternoon. Through this book, Chris invites you to join him as well. Rarely is the wisdom of a theologian of such caliber this accessible. So grab your Bible, pull up a seat, and explore what the Scripture has to say about life in the Spirit."

Lindsay Olesberg, author of *The Bible Study Handbook*

"Prepare for those 'aha!' moments and a few shouts of 'of course!' as Chris Wright takes us on a biblical journey, straightforward and deep, into the fruit of the Spirit. With his characteristic balance of profundity and simplicity, Chris Wright offers a stirring view of the transforming impact of Scripture as it reveals the fruit of the Spirit. And Chris roots us in the whole understanding of these dynamic truths by connecting the fruit of the Spirit with needed yet often overlooked context from the Old Testament. Encouragement jumps out from the pages of this book as readers are reminded of how our ordinary lives bear the mark of Christ's love and how giants of the faith like John Stott applied such truth via daily prayer to 'cause your fruit to ripen in my life.'"

Benjamin K. Homan, president, Langham Partnership USA
(formerly John Stott Ministries)

All Chris Wright's royalties from this book have been irrevocably assigned to Langham Literature (formerly the Evangelical Literature Trust). Langham Literature is a program of the Langham Partnership International (LPI), founded by John Stott. Chris Wright is the International Ministries Director. Langham Literature distributes evangelical books to pastors, theological students, and seminary libraries in the Majority World, and fosters the writing and publishing of Christian literature in many regional languages. For further information on Langham Literature and LPI, visit langham.org.

CULTIVATING
THE FRUIT OF THE SPIRIT

GROWING IN CHRISTLIKENESS

CHRISTOPHER J. H. WRIGHT

IVP Books

An imprint of InterVarsity Press
Downers Grove, Illinois

InterVarsity Press
P.O. Box 1400, Downers Grove, IL 60515-1426
ivpress.com
email@ivpress.com

©2017 by Christopher J. H. Wright

Published in the United States of America by InterVarsity Press, Downers Grove, Illinois, with permission from Langham Partnership. Published in the United Kingdom as Becoming Like Jesus: Cultivating the Fruit of the Spirit.

InterVarsity Press® is the book-publishing division of InterVarsity Christian Fellowship/USA®, a movement of students and faculty active on campus at hundreds of universities, colleges and schools of nursing in the United States of America, and a member movement of the International Fellowship of Evangelical Students. For information about local and regional activities, visit intervarsity.org.

All Scripture quotations, unless otherwise indicated, are taken from THE HOLY BIBLE, NEW INTERNATIONAL VERSION®, NIV® Copyright © 1973, 1978, 1984, 2011 by Biblica, Inc.™ Used by permission. All rights reserved worldwide.

While any stories in this book are true, some names and identifying information may have been changed to protect the privacy of individuals.

Cover design: David Fassett
Interior design: Beth McGill
Images: dove illustration: © martin951/iStockphoto
    graphic tree illustration: © CSA Images/Getty Images

ISBN 978-0-8308-4498-2 (print)
ISBN 978-0-8308-9133-7 (digital)

Printed in the United States of America ∞

 As a member of the Green Press Initiative, InterVarsity Press is committed to protecting the environment and to the responsible use of natural resources. To learn more, visit greenpressinitiative.org.

Library of Congress Cataloging-in-Publication Data

Names: Wright, Christopher J. H., 1947- author.
Title: Cultivating the fruit of the spirit : growing in Christlikeness /
    Christopher J.H. Wright.
Description: Downers Grove : InterVarsity Press, 2017. | Includes
    bibliographical references.
Identifiers: LCCN 2016046180 (print) | LCCN 2016046926 (ebook) | ISBN
    9780830844982 (pbk. : alk. paper) | ISBN 9780830891337 (eBook)
Subjects: LCSH: Fruit of the Spirit. | Spiritual life--Christianity. |
    Spirituality--Christianity. | Spiritual formation.
Classification: LCC BV4501.3 .W74 2017 (print) | LCC BV4501.3 (ebook) | DDC
    234/.13--dc23
LC record available at https://lccn.loc.gov/2016046180

| P | 21 | 20 | 19 | 18 | 17 | 16 | 15 | 14 | 13 | 12 | 11 | 10 | 9 | 8 | 7 | 6 | 5 | 4 |
| Y | 34 | 33 | 32 | 31 | 30 | 29 | 28 | 27 | 26 | 25 | 24 | 23 | 22 | 21 | 20 | 19 | 18 | |

To

my wife, Liz,

and all the children

and grandchildren God has given us.

May "becoming like Jesus"

be our shared aim.

CONTENTS

PREFACE

For several years, the British medical establishment ran a public awareness campaign on the importance of including plenty of fruits and vegetables in a healthy diet. They recommended that everybody should have at least five portions of fruits or vegetables in their daily meals. The campaign was popularly known as "5-A-Day." "Have you had your 5-A-Day?" people would ask each other.

In 2013, Langham Partnership UK and Ireland, under the leadership of our then executive director, Ian Buchanan, ran a campaign to encourage people to grow in Christlikeness. Langham's vision is that Christians and churches around the world should grow in depth of spiritual maturity, and not just grow in numbers through evangelism. And that means growing to become more like Jesus. We believe that such growth in maturity comes as we feed on the word of God, particularly as it is faithfully and clearly preached in a way that makes a relevant impact on people's lives and contexts. That is why one of Langham's primary goals is to raise the standards of biblical preaching.

It was decided that the main content of the campaign would be a series of Bible studies and videos on the fruit of the Spirit in Galatians 5:22-23. This was partly because we knew that John Stott, the founder of Langham Partnership who died in 2011, prayed every morning that God the Holy Spirit would cause that fruit of the Spirit to ripen in his own life. So, since Paul lists nine items in his portrait of the fruit of the Spirit, Jonathan Lamb (who was the program director for Langham Preaching) came up with the idea of calling our campaign "9-A-Day: Becoming Like Jesus." We should be as careful every day to cultivate the nine qualities that make up the fruit of the Spirit as we are to make sure we get our five portions of fruits or vegetables every day.

The Bible studies, videos, and other supporting materials for 9-A-Day can be found and downloaded for personal or group use at http://uk.langham.org/get-involved/free-lent-study-guide and at 9aday.org.uk/the-9-fruits.

In preparation for that campaign, I undertook to preach a series of Bible expositions on the fruit of the Spirit at the Portstewart Keswick Convention in Northern Ireland (my homeland) in July 2012. Out of those expositions came the short, condensed talks that I did on video for 9-A-Day (available at the above websites), and it is those expositions that provide the basic material for the chapters of this book.

The preached origin of the material leads to two further observations. First, this really is the kind of book that you need to read with your Bible handy beside you. In every chapter I have surveyed some of the depth and breadth of biblical background to each of the words the apostle Paul mentions in his fruit of the Spirit. So there is a lot of Bible exploration as you read this book, and I hope that is enriching and encouraging.

Second, since I hope this book will be helpful to other preachers (as well as general Christian readers), I have deliberately not included much by way of illustrations and stories. That may seem strange since sermons need appropriate illustrations to help emphasize their main points and make them memorable. And certainly every one of the items in the fruit of the Spirit could be illustrated abundantly with examples and stories. But one crucial element of good preaching is that it should be not only faithful to the biblical text, but also relevant to the local context of the preacher and listeners. So I hesitated to multiply examples drawn from my own context in the UK. Rather, I drew many examples from the stories and characters in the Bible itself (especially from its main character—God himself, as he reveals himself both in the Old Testament and in the person of Jesus Christ). It is then the responsibility of any preacher who wants to use this book as a resource for their own preaching to think of examples drawn from their own cultural context, and to illustrate and apply the biblical challenge of the fruit of the Spirit in a way that engages and impacts the hearts, minds, and lives of their own people.

INTRODUCTION

Heavenly Father, I pray that this day I may live in your
presence and please you more and more.
Lord Jesus, I pray that this day I may take up my cross and
follow you.
Holy Spirit, I pray that this day you will fill me with yourself
and cause your fruit to ripen in my life: love, joy, peace,
patience, kindness, goodness, faithfulness, gentleness,
and self-control.

That was the prayer that John Stott prayed every day when he first
woke up in the morning. It hardly seems surprising, then, that many
people who knew John Stott personally said that he was the most
Christlike person they ever met. For God answered his daily prayer by
making the fruit of the Spirit ripen in his life. And what the Spirit of
God does, above all, is to make those who put their faith in Jesus to
become more and more like the Jesus they love, trust, and follow. In fact,
we could say that the nine-fold fruit of the Spirit in Galatians 5:22-23
is a beautiful picture of Jesus. For of course Jesus himself was filled with
the Spirit of God, and it is Christ who dwells within us through the
Spirit. So the more we are filled with God's Spirit, and the more the
Spirit ripens his fruit within us, the more we will become like Christ.

That was the prayer of the apostle Paul too. We don't know if, like Stott, he expressed any such prayer every day for himself, but it was certainly what he longed to see happening for others he had led to faith in Christ. Paul felt like a mother to the Galatian believers, about which he says, "For whom I am again in the pains of childbirth *until Christ is formed in you*" (Gal 4:19; emphasis mine). Paul longed that Christian believers should be so filled with the Holy Spirit that Christ himself would actually be shaping their whole lives from the inside out. And that is exactly what Paul means when he comes to talk about the fruit of the Spirit in chapter 5.

But since the famous verses about the fruit of the Spirit come in Galatians 5, we need to step back a bit and see something of the context and background to what Paul says here. Then we will be able to see that his beautiful picture of fruit stands in stark contrast to two other things that are much less attractive—two things that are, rather, to be rejected altogether by those who are followers of Jesus.

Paul had been sent out by the church in Antioch to preach the good news about Jesus among the Gentiles (non-Jews) in the provinces of Asia Minor (what is now modern Turkey). We read the story in Acts 13–14. People in several towns in the region of Galatia had responded to Paul's preaching. They had become believers in Jesus of Nazareth as Lord and Savior, as the one promised by God in the Old Testament Scriptures (which Paul would have had to explain to these people since they were not Jews and knew nothing about "the Old Testament"). Paul clearly taught them about the God of Israel and how God had made that great promise to Abraham. God had promised Abraham that through him and his descendants "all peoples on earth" would find blessing (Gen 12:1-3). We know that Paul had taught his new converts about these great scriptural promises because he refers to them very clearly in his letter to them—the letter we know as "the epistle to the Galatians." Paul had assured these Galatian believers that by putting their faith in the Messiah, Jesus, they had in fact become part of God's people. They too were children of Abraham—not by becoming Jews (culturally or ethnically, or by proselyte conversion)—but by becoming children of God, adopted into God's family by God's grace and through faith in Jesus the Messiah. Though they were Gentiles, they had now become part of God's covenant people. They were included among the spiritual seed of Abraham. Essentially, Paul tells them, if you are in Christ then you are in Abraham, and God's promises are for you. Here is how he explains it:

> Understand, then, that those who have faith are children of Abraham. Scripture foresaw that God would justify the Gentiles by faith, and announced the gospel in advance to Abraham: "All nations will be blessed through you." So those who rely on faith are blessed along with Abraham, the man of faith. . . .
>
> So in Christ Jesus you are all children of God through faith, for all of you who were baptized into Christ have clothed yourselves with Christ. There is neither Jew nor Gentile, neither slave nor free, nor is there male and female, for you are all one in Christ Jesus. If you belong to Christ, then you are Abraham's seed, and heirs according to the promise. (Gal 3:7-9, 26-29)

That is what Paul had taught them, and that is what he reminds them of in this letter.

But something had happened.

Since Paul had first brought these Galatians to faith in Jesus and planted a church among them, others had come to them with a different message. These were Jews, like Paul himself. And probably they were also believers in Jesus—like the people we read about in Acts 15:5, who were former Pharisees (also like Paul). But unlike Paul, they did not think that it was enough for these Gentiles to put their faith in Jesus. No, they said that if these Gentiles wanted the blessings of the promises that God had made to Abraham, then they must join the people of Abraham by becoming Jewish proselytes. Proselytes were

Gentiles who converted to the Jewish faith by being circumcised and observing the law of Moses, including especially laws regarding the Sabbath day and eating only ritually clean food according to Jewish custom. So these other teachers were trying to persuade the Galatian believers that, in addition to their faith in Jesus Christ, they must also become, in effect, circumcised and Torah-keeping Jews.

Paul reacts very strongly. Throughout the first four chapters of his letter, he insists that Christ is all they need. Our salvation comes through faith in God's promise, just as it did for Abraham. The law given by Moses had its right and proper function for the Old Testament people of Israel during that era before Christ. But now that the Messiah has come, the way is open for people of *any* nation to experience the blessing of Abraham through faith in the Messiah Jesus. So all those who trust in Christ—whether Jew or Gentile—are freed from the obligation to live under the disciplinary authority of Old Testament law. Rather, they should live their lives in freedom, living for God, with Christ living within them, and "walking" by the Spirit.

But wouldn't this lead to moral license? That is, if people are not restrained by the law of Moses, then won't everybody—all these new Gentile believers—just do whatever they want and fall back into their old pagan immorality? No, says Paul. That is a false polarization between two extremes. These are the two dangers we referred to above, and can now name—the extremes of legalism on the one hand and license on the other.

Now, it is important to realize that the Old Testament law itself was certainly not legalism. On the contrary it was founded on God's saving grace, given to the people after God had redeemed them out of Egypt. But it could easily be *distorted* into a rather legalistic way of thinking. Those who insisted that Christians should also observe the Torah were saying that what really matters is keeping all the rules and regulations of the law (especially circumcision, the food laws, and Sabbath-keeping) as a kind of proof of your ethnic and covenantal identity, a badge to show that you were among God's righteous people, a true Jew in every sense (just as Paul had claimed he was in Phil 3:4-6).

But the answer to that distorted insistence on the law is not to swing to the opposite extreme and think that since you are not "under the law" then you can just do as you please and indulge every desire you have. Legalism at one extreme (keep all the rules) and license at the other (reject any rules) are both completely wrong answers to the question of how Christians should live.

It is surprising how both of these extremes and dangers are still found in the church today. On the one hand, there are some very legalistic Christians and churches. They stress the importance of keeping all the rules. They insist that you must do this and never do that if you want to prove you are really a Christian. They like everything to be strict and clear, and usually have very little sympathy with those who don't or won't conform. "If you can't keep our rules you aren't one of us," seems to be their attitude. On the other hand, and often in reaction against that kind of legalism, there are those who reject the whole idea of rules or traditions in the church. The whole point of the Christian faith, as they see it, is to set us free from the institutionalized religious burden. "God loves us as we are!" they say. So they have no place for concepts such as discipline or obedience. And this can lead them into the temptations of immorality; they may end up being no different from the surrounding world in the way they live and think.

So we seem to swing between the law-enforcers and the rule-rejecters, but this is a completely mistaken and false polarity. And Paul addresses it in Galatians 5. He shows us a far better way—the truly Christian way to live our lives—the way of the Spirit of God given to us through Christ.

First of all, Paul agrees that, yes, the gospel of Christ has indeed set us free. So he urges the Galatians not to give in to those who wanted to impose the whole Old Testament law on them so that they could base their righteousness on that law by having an acquired Jewish identity. "It is for freedom that Christ has set us free. Stand firm, then, and do not let yourselves be burdened again by a yoke of slavery" (Gal 5:1).

Since they had trusted in the Messiah Jesus, it did not matter if they were circumcised or not; what mattered was that their faith was real and was proving its reality by their love. "For in Christ Jesus neither circumcision nor uncircumcision has any value. The only thing that counts is faith expressing itself through love" (Gal 5:6).

But then immediately Paul insists that being "free" does not mean freedom to indulge "the flesh." In Paul's writing, "the flesh" does not simply mean our physical human bodies, but rather it is shorthand for our fallen, sinful, human nature (which includes our bodies, of course, but also embraces our thoughts, emotions, will, desires, feelings, etc.). "You, my brothers and sisters, were called to be free. But do not use your freedom to indulge the flesh; rather, serve one another humbly in love" (Gal 5:13).

Did you notice that double reference to *love* at the end of both verses 6 and 13 (and another one coming up in verse 14)? Love is the answer to both legalism and license.

To the law-enforcers Paul says that what really matters is faith expressing itself *through love*. Love enables us to fulfill God's law properly without legalism.

And to the rule-rejecters Paul says that we should make sure that we serve one another humbly *in love*. Love enables us to use our freedom properly without selfishness.

Let me explain both those points further. On the one hand, love for one another is the right way to respond obediently and faithfully to God's law, as God himself intended and as Jesus pointed out. Paul echoes Jesus in Galatians 5:14 by quoting Leviticus 19:18: "For the entire law is fulfilled in keeping this one command: 'Love your neighbor as yourself"" (see also Rom 13:9-10). For that is the verse that Jesus had called the second great commandment in the law after the first commandment, which is "Love the LORD your God with all your heart and with all your soul and with all your strength" (Deut 6:5).

On the other hand, love will prevent us from using our freedom for selfish indulgence. Christian freedom, while it releases us from one kind of slavery (submitting to the law), actually puts us into a very different kind of slavery for Christ's sake—submitting to one another by serving one another humbly in love.

No wonder Paul puts love at the head of the list of the fruit of the Spirit a few verses later in Galatians 5:22. It is *doubly* important!

And then, just before moving to the climax of his argument, Paul throws in a warning to *both* groups. Law-enforcers and rule-rejecters can be pretty horrible to each other in attitudes and words—spoken and written. They can end up like fighting dogs, tearing pieces out of each other, and that kind of conflict between Christians can end up destroying a church completely. Watch out, says Paul. "If you bite and devour each other, watch out or you will be destroyed by each other" (Gal 5:15).

At last Paul comes to his big point. If we should not be governed by either the law or the flesh, then what *should* govern how we live? Answer: the Spirit. Paul puts this at the beginning, middle, and end of his next section in verses 16, 18, and 25: "Walk by the Spirit . . . led by the Spirit . . . live by the Spirit . . . keep in step with the Spirit." That is the heart and soul of Christian living. It is the center and secret of what it means to be a person in Christ.

And just as Paul has spoken about *the power of love* to enable us both to live in a right relationship to Old Testament law and to overcome the selfishness of the flesh, so also Paul now explains that if we allow *the power of the Spirit of God* to govern the way we live, we will avoid both of those extremes of legalism and license. That is what he explains in verses 16 through 18:

So I say, walk by the Spirit, and you will not gratify the desires of the flesh. For the flesh desires what is contrary to the
Spirit, and the Spirit what is contrary to the flesh. They are
in conflict with each other, so that you are not to do whatever
you want. But if you are led by the Spirit, you are not under
the law. (Gal 5:16-18)

So when we say "Yes" to Jesus Christ, and "Yes" to the Holy Spirit,
we say "No" to the flesh (we will not just do whatever we want), and
we say "No" to those who want to bring us under the burden of the
law as a way of proving our own righteousness.

Now, at this point we want to hurry on and find out what it means
to walk, live and be led by the Spirit, but Paul wants to make sure, first
of all, that we are very clear about the opposite. What kind of life do
the "acts of the flesh" lead to? Paul gives a somber list in verses 19
through 21:

The acts of the flesh are obvious: sexual immorality, impurity and
debauchery; idolatry and witchcraft; hatred, discord, jealousy,
fits of rage, selfish ambition, dissensions, factions and envy;
drunkenness, orgies, and the like. I warn you, as I did before, that
those who live like this will not inherit the kingdom of God.
(Gal 5:19-21)

It is dark, but revealing. It mentions things that are individual, and
things that are social and cultural. It ranges from private to public,
from outward acts to inward emotions. And it is a true reflection of
what we see all around us, to a greater or lesser extent. This is the
world we live in. And it is the world we are called to be different from.
But how?

So now at last, and in dazzling contrast to that list, Paul describes
the life of the Spirit. Here is the passage that will be our text throughout
the rest of this book:

But the fruit of the Spirit is love, joy, peace, patience, kindness, goodness, faithfulness, gentleness and self-control. Against such things there is no law. (Gal 5:22-23 NIV 1984)

Let's notice first what this text is *not*. It is not a list of virtues, matching the list of vices just listed as "acts of the flesh." In Greek and Jewish texts from that time, there were common matching lists of vices and virtues that were supposed to shape people's behavior. Basically they said, "Don't do these things (the vices). Rather, do these things (the virtues)." In either case, the emphasis was on *what you should not do* and *what you should do instead*. Of course, there is some similarity with Paul's double listing here. But lists of vices and virtues could also easily be used simply as lists of rules—"don't do this list" and "do this list." And that is definitely *not* what Paul is talking about here. Paul is not saying, "Don't try to obey all the rules in the Old Testament law; here is a much easier set of rules to obey instead." That would be to replace one wrong attitude with another one. Paul is not really talking about rules at all.

No, the key to understanding what Paul is saying here lies in the metaphor he uses—fruit. All the lovely words he writes are, taken altogether, the *fruit* (singular) *of the Spirit*. Now fruit is the natural product of life. If a tree is alive, it will bear fruit. That is the nature of being a living tree! Fruit is what you get when a tree has life within it.

Why does a tree bear fruit? Not because there is some law of nature that says it must. But simply because of the life within it, rising up from the soil and water that feed its roots and flowing in the sap through every branch and twig. A tree does not bear fruit by keeping the laws of nature (if we can use our imagination and think like a tree), but simply because it is a living tree, being and doing what a tree is and does when it is alive.

So what Paul is saying with his list of beautiful qualities is this: these are the qualities that God himself will produce in a person's everyday, ordinary human life because the life of God himself is at work within them. The life of God (by his Spirit) will bear fruit in the tree of a person's life, simply because this is what God is like and this is what God produces. Or, as we said above, the Spirit of God, which is the Spirit of Christ, will make the qualities of the life of Christ grow in a person's life, so that they become more and more like Christ— which is God's desire for all his children.

What Paul is talking about here is Christian *character*. Character is, sadly, greatly undervalued today in so much church life and activity. We'd rather work out the best techniques, formulate successful strategies, and celebrate (or criticize) performance. We look on the outside and assess people by "how they are doing," and pay much less attention to what kind of character they have become or are becoming. But look at the qualities in Paul's list of the fruit of the Spirit. They do not focus on what kind of *performance* we can achieve, but what kind of *person* we are.

Fruit takes time. Character takes time—a lifetime, in fact. John Stott was praying that prayer daily throughout his life. So, let us then take the time to study the fruit in the orchard of God's Spirit, and then take the time to let that fruit ripen in our own lives, through all the time God gives us.

Watch a video from Chris about the fruit of the Spirit
at **ivpress.com/cultivating-intro.**

1

LOVE

First up—love.

And that's not surprising, really. Paul has already made the point that what really matters is "faith expressing itself through love" (Gal 5:6), *and* that we should be serving "one another humbly in love" (Gal 5:13), and that the whole Old Testament law is summed up in the commandment "love your neighbor as yourself" (Gal 5:14).

In putting love first, Paul is echoing Jesus. In the book of Matthew, when someone asked Jesus about the greatest commandment in the law, he responded with two, one from Deuteronomy and one from Leviticus:

> Jesus replied: "Love the Lord your God with all your heart and with all your soul and with all your mind." This is the first and greatest commandment. And the second is like it: "Love your neighbor as yourself." All the Law and the Prophets hang on these two commandments. (Mt 22:37-40, quoting Deut 6:5 and Lev 19:18)

Almost certainly, it is that second kind of love—neighbor love—that Paul means by the fruit of the Spirit here. That is, he means that the first fruit of the Spirit is not so much our love for God, but our love for one another as Christians—across all our differences and barriers. And Paul is talking about not just sentimental feelings of being nice, but real practical proof that we love and accept one another, in down-to-earth caring, providing, helping, encouraging, and supporting one another, even when it costs a lot or hurts a lot to do so. Love in action, in other words. Love that dissolves divisions. Love that brings together people who would otherwise hate, hurt, and even kill one another.

Just how important is loving one another in that way? Why is it very first in Paul's list of the fruit of the Spirit? Paul himself had plenty to say about the importance of Christians loving one another, but it is John who emphasizes it more than any other New Testament writer.

So let's turn to John as our guide for this first study. *Three* times in his Gospel, John records Jesus telling his disciples that he commanded them to love one another:

> "A new command I give you: Love one another. As I have loved you, so you must love one another. By this everyone will know that you are my disciples, if you love one another." (Jn 13:34-35)

> My command is this: Love each other as I have loved you. (Jn 15:12)

> This is my command: Love each other. (Jn 15:17)

Five times in his first letter, John reminds us that this is God's command, and goes into a lot of detail about how we should love one another not just in words but also with actions and in truth:

> For this is the message you heard from the beginning: We should love one another. (1 Jn 3:11)

> If anyone has material possessions and sees a brother or sister in need but has no pity on them, how can the love of God be in that person? Dear children, let us not love with words or speech but with actions and in truth. (1 Jn 3:17-18)

"homeless"

And this is his command: to believe in the name of his Son, Jesus Christ, and to love one another as he commanded us. (1 Jn 3:23)

Dear friends, let us love one another, for love comes from God. Everyone who loves has been born of God and knows God. Whoever does not love does not know God, because God is love. (1 Jn 4:7-8)

Dear friends, since God so loved us, we also ought to love one another. No one has ever seen God; but if we love one another, God lives in us and his love is made complete in us. (1 Jn 4:11-12)

So if anything can be said to be primary, central, and essential to being a Christian and becoming more like Jesus, it must be this. That is why Paul speaks of this kind of love as the first evidence that God is at work in our lives, the first fruit of the Spirit of God within us. John too sees such love as *evidence*. It proves something. In fact, love proves several things that we can look at together. When Christians love one another, says John, it is evidence of some very important realities: love is evidence of life, evidence of faith, evidence of God, and evidence for Jesus.

Love for One Another Is the Evidence of Life

John wants to reassure the church community he was writing to that they were true believers and that they shared the life of God, eternal life. So John takes his readers back to the very foundations of their faith to the teaching they heard from the very beginning, when they first heard the gospel and responded to it.

Twice John uses the words, "This is the message we [you] have heard." The first time is in 1 John 1:5: "This is the message we have heard from him and declare to you: God is light; in him there is no darkness at all."

Then, halfway through his letter, John repeats that phrase, links it to what he has just said about doing what is right, and then expands it with the command to love one another. "Anyone who does not do what is right is not God's child, nor is anyone who does not love their brother and sister. For this is the message you heard from the beginning: We should love one another" (1 Jn 3:10-11).

For John, *walking in the light* and *walking in love* were together the two most basic and essential parts of being a true Christian. They were part of the original message and teaching of Jesus himself ("from the beginning"). And they were part of the gospel that they had heard and believed.

But then John goes even further. He makes another of his frequent "we know" statements. John insists that we *can* and *should* know some very important things in our Christian life. And here is possibly the most important thing we can know. We can *know* that we have eternal life. We can be sure about that. In fact, John tells us that that is the prime reason why he wrote his Gospel (John 20:30-31), and also the reason why he wrote his letter (1 Jn 5:13).

So John wanted his readers to know for sure that they had eternal life. But how can you know you've got the life that God gives? When you see the evidence of the love that God produces in your life. "We know that we have passed from death to life, because we love each other. Anyone who does not love remains in death" (1 Jn 3:14).

Christian love is a matter of life and death. It's as serious as that. It's what proves you have passed from one to the other.

Now that verse (1 Jn 3:14) is very similar to something Jesus said: "Whoever hears my word and *believes* him who sent me *has eternal life*" (Jn 5:24, emphasis mine). So it is when we respond to Jesus and put our faith in God through him that we receive eternal life (says Jesus). But it is when we love one another that we *know* we have passed from death to life, because we see the evidence (says John). Faith in God through Jesus and love for one another as Christians— these two hang together. Our eternal life is received by faith and demonstrated by love.

How do you know if a tree is alive? You look for the buds, the leaves, and then the fruit. The fruit is the evidence that the tree has life within it. Where there is fruit, there is life. But if there's no fruit, the tree may be dead.

How do you know if a believer, or a church, is alive? Look for the love. Where there is love, there is life. When Christians truly put love into practice, it is evidence, assurance, that the life of God is present among them and in them. But when we don't put love into practice, when we fight and squabble, divide and denounce each other . . . what does it say about us? If there's no love, says John, we have not come to life at all; we "remain in death."

Love is a life and death thing.

To reinforce how important this is, John gives us two examples— one on each side of his central point in 1 John 3:14.

The negative example: Cain (1 Jn 3:12, 15). Cain was filled with hatred, and hatred led to death. That is the way it goes. So verse 15 gives a very severe warning: hatred of a fellow Christian is like murder (again John is echoing Jesus from Mt 5:21-22). If people claim to be Christians, but their lives, attitudes, and words are filled with hatred of others, then John warns us that they may not even have eternal life at all, no matter what they claim.

The positive example: Christ (1 Jn 3:16). Christ was filled with love, and his love led him to *give* his life (not to take life, as Cain did). So the essence of love is self-sacrifice for others. That's how Jesus himself described his coming death as the good shepherd (Jn 10:11, 15). And as Paul put it, "God demonstrates his own love for us in this: While we were still sinners, Christ died for us" (Rom 5:8).

So, says John, don't be like Cain (not even in your thoughts). Be like Christ (not only in your thoughts, but in practical life, 1 Jn 3:18).

And then, just in case we might imagine that the principle of self-sacrifice, of laying down our lives for others (1 Jn 3:16), is only for those rare and extreme moments when we might actually have to *die* for somebody else, John immediately illustrates what he means in verse 17. He's talking about the simple, ordinary, everyday opportunities to show real practical generosity, care, and kindness. "If anyone has material possessions and sees a brother or sister in need but has no pity on them, *how can the love of God be in that person?*" (1 Jn 3:17, emphasis mine). That's a powerful rhetorical question, expecting the answer: "It can't be—no matter what the person claims." We can't claim to love God, or that God's love is within us, if we don't help the needy when we have the ability to do so. Well, we *may* claim to love God, but it's simply a lie—as John later says with devastating logic, "Whoever claims to love God yet hates a brother or sister is a liar. For whoever does not love their brother and sister, whom they have seen, cannot love God, whom they have not seen" (1 Jn 4:20).

Love for One Another Is the Evidence of Faith

The point that John makes about *love* (that it needs to be proved in action) is very similar to what James says about *faith* in this familiar passage:

> What good is it, my brothers and sisters, if someone claims to have faith but has no deeds? Can such faith save them? Suppose a brother or a sister is without clothes and daily food. If one of you says to them, "Go in peace; keep warm and well fed," but does nothing about their physical needs, what good is it? In the same way, faith by itself, if it is not accompanied by action, is dead. (Jas 2:14-17)

John would have agreed, of course—and so would Paul. But John connects faith and love in a way that makes them just as inseparable as faith and good deeds. In fact, he puts them together as a single command: "And this is his command: to believe in the name of his Son, Jesus Christ, and to love one another as he commanded us" (1 Jn 3:23).

Notice that John says, "This is his *command* (singular)." But then he goes on to state *two* things! We are commanded not only to believe in the name of God's Son, Jesus Christ, but also to love one another—and together they are one integrated command. If you do the first (believe), you will do the second (love). If you aren't doing the second (loving one another), you aren't doing the first (believing in Jesus). Don't try to split them, for they are both the *single* command of God: believe-in-Jesus-and-love-one-another. They go together.

So love for one another is not only the evidence of the life of God within us, it is also the evidence of the faith through which we came to receive that life in the first place. James said that faith without deeds is dead. John would agree by saying that faith without love (love that is proved in good deeds) is also dead—nothing but an empty claim. In fact, since "this is his command," it follows that if we aren't showing practical love for one another, we are simply disobeying the commands of the Jesus we say we believe in. And what kind of disciples are we then?

Love for One Another Is Evidence for God

One of the most famous verses in the Bible, after John 3:16, is "God is love" (1 Jn 4:8). As with all Bible verses, it's important to read it in context. Here it is in a wonderfully rich passage about love and God:

> Dear friends, let us love one another, for love comes from God. Everyone who loves has been born of God and knows God. Whoever does not love does not know God, because *God is love*. This is how God showed his love among us: He sent his one and only Son into the world that we might live through him. This is love: not that we loved God, but that he loved us and sent his Son as an atoning sacrifice for our sins. Dear friends, since God so loved us, we also ought to love one another. No one has ever seen God; but if we love one another, God lives in us and his love is made complete in us. (1 Jn 4:7-12, emphasis mine)

John says three main things in this passage.

God is the source of all love (1 Jn 4:7-8). "Love comes from God," he says. All human love flows from God because God is the source of all true love, since love is his very nature and being. This tells us something about God. God is love through and through. All that God does or says is ultimately an expression of his love. When God acts in justice, it is the expression of God's love. When God acts in anger, it is God's love defending itself (and us) from everything that would spoil and destroy the world and the people he has made in love. God's whole attitude and action towards his creation is love. Or as Psalm 145 puts it twice, the Lord "is loving toward everything he has made" (Ps 145:13, 17 NIRV). God's love is the greatest reality in the universe, greater even than the universe itself.

So, yes, this passage tells us a glorious truth about God. But remember, John is primarily talking to his readers, and his main point is that whoever does not live in love with others is not connected to God, who is the source of love. Indeed, such a person does not really know God at all and is not a child of God.

God has given us the proof and model of his love (1 Jn 4:9-11). John comes back to the very heart of the gospel itself. How do we know that God loves us? Because God the Father gave his only Son, and God the Son willingly gave himself, to save us from eternal death and give us eternal life. The wonderful truth of the gospel of 1 John 3:16 is just beneath the surface of these verses.

The cross is the ultimate proof of God's love—the love of the Father and of the Son. Notice the beautiful balance between 1 John 4:9-10, which speaks of the love of the Father in sending his Son, and 1 John 3:16, which speaks of the love of the Son in laying down his life for us. Paul makes exactly the same balanced point when he speaks of God the Father as the one "who did not spare his own Son, but gave him up for us all" (Rom 8:32), and of "the Son of God, who loved me and gave himself for me" (Gal 2:20).

But once again, remember the main point here. John is saying all this about God's love not just to teach us good atonement theology. His big point is to motivate us to *imitate* the love of God the Father and God the Son by loving one another. And so that brings us to the climax of his argument: "*Since God so loved us,* we also ought to love one another" (1 Jn 4:11, emphasis mine). The cross is not just the means by which we are saved, but also the model for how we are to live.

Peter makes the same double point. Jesus, he says, "'bore our sins' in his body on the cross" (1 Pet 2:24). That is how our sins can be forgiven, because of the atoning death of Christ. But in the same passage he writes, "Christ suffered for you, leaving you an example, that you should follow in his steps. . . . He did not retaliate; when he suffered, he made no threats" (1 Pet 2:21, 23). Similarly, says John, God's love, proved on the cross, is a model and example for us to follow. "Since God . . . we ought . . ." (1 Jn 4:11). It's as simple as that.

So then, if you're having a hard struggle to love other Christians (as often happens, for all kinds of reasons), there are two things you should do: first, go to the *source of love,* God himself, and ask for his divine love to fill you; and second, look at the *model of love,* the cross of Christ, and follow his example.

But then John goes one step further and makes an even more powerful statement about what happens when Christians love one another.

God becomes visible through our love for one another (1 Jn 4:12). "No one has ever seen God; but if we love one another, God lives in us and his love is made complete in us" (1 Jn 4:12).

"No one has ever seen God." But what about all those appearances of God in the Old Testament to people like Abraham and Moses? Well, yes, in a sense God did make himself visible to them in some temporary human form, or through an angel. Such events are called theophanies, from the Ancient Greek *theophaneia* meaning "appearance of a god." When God wanted to say or do something particularly significant at a moment of history, he would appear to someone in the story. But even then, there was a caution about speaking about seeing God. They knew that God, as God really is in himself, is invisible. God is not part of the physical world that we live in and can see around us. God is not an object. God is Spirit, the creator of the universe, not a thing or body we can see with our physical eyes. So in that sense, John truthfully says, "No one has ever seen God" (1 Jn 4:12).

But this is actually the second time John has written those exact words. The first time is in his Gospel. Right at the beginning, when he is talking about the wonder of how the eternal Word of God has entered our world of space and time, John says this: "No one has ever seen God, but the one and only Son, who is himself God and is in the closest relationship with the Father, has made him known" (Jn 1:18).

Jesus Christ, the Word who became flesh, has made God visible. God, in the person of Jesus Christ, was seen and heard and touched. In fact, John reminds the readers of his letter of this same point right at the start: "That which was from the beginning, which we have heard, which we have seen with our eyes, which we have looked at and our hands have touched—this we proclaim concerning the Word of life" (1 Jn 1:1). So yes, God who is invisible in himself, was seen in the earthly life of Jesus of Nazareth. As Jesus himself put it, "Anyone who has seen me has seen the Father" (Jn 14:9).

Well, we might say, that was all very well and good for those who did actually see Jesus when he was here living on earth. They had this wonderful opportunity of seeing the invisible God, made visible in the person and life of Jesus of Nazareth. Good for them. But what about the rest of us? What about the rest of the human race who never had the chance to see Jesus? Is there any way that God can be seen today?

Amazingly, John makes this second statement starting exactly the same way: "No one has ever seen God; *but if we love one another*, God lives in us and God's love is made complete in us" (1 Jn 4:12, emphasis mine). It seems that John is implying that our love for one another makes visible the love of God—which is another way of saying that God himself is seen, since God is love. When Christians love each other, in practical, sacrificial, costly, barrier-dissolving ways, then the love of God (or rather, the God who is love) can be seen. The world should be able to look at Christians and how they live together and love together and see something of the reality of God being demonstrated. The invisible God makes himself visible in the love that Christians have for one another.

Now of course, none of us is perfect, and all of us fail in all kinds of ways. That is why we often protect ourselves a bit when we say things like, "Don't look at me, or don't look at Christians; look at Jesus." Well, yes, we should never boast. And yes, we do want people to focus on Christ, not on ourselves. But sometimes that kind of thinking and speaking can be an excuse for not even trying to obey Christ's command to love one another. For, according to John, the world *should* be able to look at Christians and Christian churches and see something that demonstrates the reality of God. They should be able to see God in action.

And that is especially true when people who would otherwise hate and kill one another, such as people who come from nations that have a history of war with each other, can show that they love one another because of the love of God in Christ. During the Rwanda genocide in 1994, students in the IFES (International Fellowship of Evangelical Students) movement who came from the Hutu and Tutsi tribes were warned to separate from each other. But they stood in a circle, holding hands in prayer, saying, "We live together, united by Christ, and we will die together if necessary." And many of them did die together. Only the gospel of the love of God could have unified them.

We see the gospel when a Messianic Jewish Israeli and a Palestinian Christian believer can stand and embrace one another on an international platform, as they did at the Lausanne Congress in Cape Town in 2010. God himself becomes visible when God's children love one another, even though the world tells them to do the opposite.

Some years ago, the atheist societies in the UK paid for an ad to be placed on the famous red London buses. It said, "There probably is no God, so stop worrying and enjoy life." There are many Christians in London. So in theory, a non-Christian reading that ad should be able to say: "That just can't be true (that there is no God), because I know Sarah and Nirmala and Sam and Ajith, and they are Christians, and God is obviously real and living in them."

We are supposed to be the living proof of the living God. No one can see God. But people can see us. And when we love one another, it is the love of God they see.

This might all sound very positive, and it is. But we do need to stop and think about the negative effects when the opposite is true—when Christians *do not* or *will not* love one another, and instead find all kinds of ways of excusing themselves from this command of Jesus, and show no evidence of this first fruit of the Spirit.

According to John, when people who claim to be Christians show no evidence of this kind of God-like, Christ-like, Spirit-produced love, then they call into question whether they are truly born again (1 Jn 4:7); they show that they don't really know God (1 Jn 4:8); and they are despising the cross of Christ by refusing to live as if it has anything to teach us (1 Jn 4:9-10). But worst of all, they are keeping God invisible (1 Jn 4:12). They are hiding the love of God. They are concealing the God who is love, the God who cannot be seen in himself, but longs to be seen in and through us.

So for all those reasons, such people are actually frustrating God's mission and hindering people from entering the kingdom of God, in the same way that those who resisted and rejected Jesus did in the Gospel stories.

When Christians do not love one another, it is not just tragic, it is toxic. It is poisonous and deadly. It frustrates the very reason for our existence. Our mission is to be disciples and make disciples, sharing and living the good news of the gospel of the love of God by showing how it transforms our own lives and relationships.

That all comes from the first letter of John. But we can go back to Jesus himself for our conclusion.

Love for One Another Is Evidence for Jesus

Jesus said, "A new command I give you: Love one another. As I have loved you, so you must love one another. By this everyone will know that you are my disciples, if you love one another" (Jn 13:34-35).

When Christians love each other, it shows who they belong to. It points people to Jesus. Christian love is incredibly transforming, and in many contexts so surprising and countercultural that it can only be the work of Christ, the power of the gospel, the fruit of the Spirit.

What a vital fruit this kind of love is! It is absolutely first and foremost. When Christians love one another, it proves they have eternal life and a saving faith, it proves the reality of God, and it proves that they are true followers of Jesus. But when they don't . . . well, what does that prove?

Questions

1. What Bible stories illustrate the theme of love?

2. What examples can you give from your own cultural context or history that illustrate the power of love to prove the truth of the gospel, for example, in the reconciling of enemies?

3. What evidence is there of either the presence or the absence of love as the fruit of God's Spirit?

Watch a video from Chris about love at
ivpress.com/cultivating-love.

2

JOY

Love, joy, and peace—the first three on Paul's list of the fruit of the Spirit—are like a triplet. They come together. Jesus linked them very closely in his farewell conversations with his disciples:

> *Peace* I leave with you; my peace I give you. I do not give to you as the world gives. Do not let your hearts be troubled and do not be afraid. (John 14:27, emphasis mine)

> As the Father has loved me, so have I loved you. Now remain in my *love*. If you keep my commands, you will remain in my love, just as I have kept my Father's commands and remain in his love. (John 15:9-10, emphasis mine)

> I have told you this so that my *joy* may be in you and that your joy may be complete. (John 15:11, emphasis mine)

And, to continue the picture, joy and peace are like twins. They come together as a pair even more often than love, joy, and peace come as a triplet. And Paul is particularly fond of the two words, joy and peace. This is the kind of thing he loves to say:

> For the kingdom of God is not a matter of eating and drinking, but of righteousness, *peace and joy* in the Holy Spirit. (Rom 14:17, emphasis mine)

May the God of hope fill you with all *joy and peace* as you trust in him, so that you may overflow with hope by the power of the Holy Spirit. (Rom 15:13, emphasis mine)

In fact, Paul speaks of joy twenty-one times and peace forty-three times in his letters! But we can see in those verses in Romans that for Paul, joy and peace are not just incidental byproducts of the Christian faith. They are not just happy feelings. Look at what else he says about them in just those few verses above—it's an impressive list.

- Joy and peace are key signs of the kingdom of God, just as important as righteousness. These are things that happen when God reigns—true joy and peace are born.

- Joy and peace are the way we are to serve and please God—not in solemn anxiety.

- Joy and peace are essential ingredients in our Christian hope—we are to be *filled* with joy and peace.

- Joy and peace are evidence of the power of the Holy Spirit overflowing in our lives.

So it's not surprising that he includes joy and peace in the fruit of the Spirit! These words are not just describing a cheerful, contented emotional state. This is something profound and at the heart of our Christian life and witness.

Let's think first of joy. What brings you joy? What makes your eyes sparkle? What makes your heart leap up and down? What gives you a glow of pleasure and makes you smile, laugh, or whoop out loud and throw your arms up in the air for joy and want to hug everybody around you?

When I ask myself that question, four things come to mind very quickly, and each of them connects with something very true about Christian joy as the fruit of the Spirit. These four things bring me great joy (even if I don't do all the things I just mentioned—though sometimes you might just see me behaving like that!): having a family, having a feast, having a faith, and having a future.

Joy is having a family. Joy fills me when I'm with my family sharing the love that binds us all together, or with close friends when I just enjoy being in their company for a meal or a drink. Or when I open our front door and see the happy faces of our grandchildren, jumping up and down with excitement. Or just when I'm out for a day with my wife. (If you think that is unfair to those who don't have a family, just wait a moment).

Joy is having a feast. This sort of joy springs up when I get really good news, particularly if it was unexpected or anxiously waited for. Then joy turns to celebration. I remember when the telegram arrived to say that I'd got a place at Cambridge, after all the study and anxiety. Or the day (place and time etched in my memory) when I asked Elizabeth Brown to marry me, and she said "Yes" (not that there was much anxiety—we'd been going together for years). Or the joy of getting news that a loved one had come safely through a surgical operation or recovered from serious illness. Or the news that our daughters were pregnant, and then the news (in each case) that a healthy baby was born and all was well with them both. When there's really good news, we celebrate it with joy, as we do for birthdays and anniversaries. Many cultures celebrate such moments by having a great party-meal. We mark moments of joy with food and drink.

Joy is having a faith. Sometimes I am filled with intense joy when I am in church worshiping God with other Christians. Mind you, there are other times when that can be a rather miserable experience (unfortunately). But there are moments when the words of the Scriptures or the music and words of certain hymns and songs are so rich, when they remind me so powerfully of what God has done to save me, that my heart almost bursts with joy. I know deep down that I could not be what I am, or where I am, apart from the forgiving grace and daily embracing love of God. And when the worship, especially the music, reminds me of that, there are times I cannot sing because my eyes fill up with tears of joy and my voice is choked up with gratitude to God.

Joy is having a future. I often bubble up with joy when I'm out enjoying God's creation. I love the pleasure of being alive in God's world. I feel joy in just being able to run or walk out in the open air, or go for a swim in the sea or a lake. It's a joy that, for me, is stuffed full of gratitude to God. This is God's world and I love it and enjoy it—as God meant us to—and as the Psalms celebrate with great joy. But there is another part of that joy, and it is knowing that this creation we now enjoy so much is only the womb—the groaning womb—of the new creation. So we look forward, not just to "going to heaven," but to our resurrection bodies in the new heaven and earth that God is creating. What joy that will be! And it will be forever! Wow!

All four of these reasons for joy in ordinary life are true in even greater ways of the joy that fills the life and heart of a Christian as the fruit of the Spirit. Let's take them in turn.

Joy Is Having a Family

Let's go back to those verses in Romans (quoted above), where Paul prays that his readers would be filled with joy and peace. The Christians at Rome were a mixture of Jews who had come to believe in Jesus as Messiah, and Gentiles who had come from a completely "outside," pagan background. And Paul has spent two chapters (Romans 14 and 15) telling them to accept and welcome one another, because God in Christ had accepted them and made them into one people. Then Paul quotes several Old Testament texts that called on the Gentiles to praise and rejoice in what God has done (Rom 15:9-12). The second quotation says, "Rejoice, you Gentiles, with his people" (Rom 15:10, quoting Deut 32:43).

Why did Paul tell the Gentile Christians at Rome to rejoice? What did they have to be joyful about? They should be filled with joy because they were now included in a whole new family—they belonged to God's own people ("rejoice *with* his people," emphasis mine). They were no longer far away, outside in the cold, but included. They had a whole new set of relationships because of the Lord Jesus Christ and his reconciling death and resurrection.

Paul made this point even more emphatically to the Gentile Christians in Ephesus. First he reminded them of what they used to be, before they came to faith in Jesus: "Remember that at that time you were separate from Christ, excluded from citizenship in Israel and foreigners to the covenants of the promise, without hope and without God in the world" (Eph 2:12).

They were alienated in every possible way. They did not belong to the people of God and they knew nothing about the love and redemption and covenant promises of the God of Israel. They had no relationship with God or God's people. They did not belong to the family of God. Not a very joyful place to be.

But Paul says that now things have completely changed: "But now in Christ Jesus you who once were far away have been brought near by the blood of Christ. . . . Consequently, you are no longer foreigners and strangers, but fellow citizens with God's people and also members of his household" (Eph 2:13, 19).

Those who were far away have been brought near. Those who were on the outside have been brought in. Those who were excluded from the family are now included as family members. The Gentiles have become not only citizens of God's people (a political metaphor), but members of God's household (a family metaphor). And a little later Paul will add that they have also become the place of God's dwelling through the Holy Spirit (Eph 2:22; a temple metaphor). That is surely a good reason for joy! Christian believers, no matter what their background or circumstances, get a whole new family through belonging to Christ.

Maybe, earlier on in this chapter, you didn't like the way I started my list of things that give me joy by mentioning my family. We all know that there are so many people who, sadly, have very little joy, or no joy at all, from having a family. There are all kinds of reasons for that: cruel parents, marriage breakups, lonely singleness, bereavement, feuds, hatreds, and even persecution by non-Christian family members. But when people belong to Christ, even if they do not have the joy of a vibrant and loving human family, or even if they endure the pain of a broken and abusive family, or loneliness, or bereavement—when they belong to Christ they have the joy of a new family among God's people. This does not mean that everything is nice and rosy suddenly. It does not necessarily mend all the brokenness or fix all the problems. But there is a joy in belonging to the family of God through Jesus Christ in the midst of the sorrow and pain and struggle of a dysfunctional or missing human family. This is a joy that is deeper than just feeling happy because everything is going well. It is a joy that comes from knowing you are part of a family you can never lose, part of the oldest family in history, the largest family on earth, and your family for all eternity. These family relationships are created and shared because Jesus brings the joy that is the fruit of the Spirit.

Two stories filled with joy can illustrate this. When the Prodigal Son in Jesus' parable returned home, he was embraced and welcomed back into the family by his father—even though he had effectively renounced his family by going off with his inheritance to a far country. And there was great joy and celebration. Jesus told this story, along with the one about the lost sheep and the lost coin, to make the point that the joy of being found and brought back is shared not just by the animal, coin, or boy, but by God and the angels in heaven (Lk 15:7, 10). There is joy in heaven, not just on earth!

And then there was the Ethiopian eunuch in Acts 8. As a eunuch, he could obviously not have a family, sons and daughters of his own. But he had come to Jerusalem to worship the God of Israel, just as Solomon had prayed foreigners would do (1 Kings 8:41-43). And he had purchased a scroll of the book of Isaiah. He was reading the verses that we now call Isaiah 53, about how the Servant of the Lord would be slain for our sins. Philip explains that passage to him and leads him to faith in Jesus. But I like to imagine that Philip then pointed the Ethiopian to the nearby passage that we find in Isaiah 56 where God had made a promise to eunuchs, who could have no children:

> To them I will give within my temple and its walls
>> a memorial and a name
>> better than sons and daughters;
> I will give them an everlasting name
>> that will endure forever. (Is 56:5)

In other words, even if they could not have a family of their own, God would bring them into his own family, whose family name would never die out.

And a little later, God adds that when he brings eunuchs and foreigners to worship him and belong to him then, "these I will bring to my holy mountain and give them joy in my house of prayer" (Is 56:7).

Well, this Ethiopian had been to the holy mountain and to the temple, God's house of prayer. But it was when he heard the good news about Jesus, trusted in him, and was baptized by Philip, that Luke tells us, "he went on his way *rejoicing*" (Acts 8:39, emphasis mine). He went back to Africa, to his job in the government of the Queen of Ethiopia, but he now had a new family because he belonged to Jesus. So he went back with joy. In fact he not only took the gospel with him to Africa, but he was the first person in the book of Acts from outside the Jewish nation in the land of Judah and Samaria to become part of the multinational family of God in the Messiah Jesus. What joy that is (especially if you're African)!

Joy Is Having a Feast

Joy, as part of the fruit of the Spirit, is a New Testament word, of course, and as we've seen, Paul uses it a lot. But it is also prominent in the Old Testament. In fact, the people of Israel were *commanded* to rejoice and be joyful! So many of their songs in the book of Psalms call on the people to celebrate, sing, rejoice, praise, give thanks, etc. Joy is very much in the air (alongside some very serious lament and protest too, of course, since life could sometimes be as tough for them as it can be for us).

There were three annual festivals in Israel—Passover along with the Feast of Unleavened Bread, The Feast of Weeks (Pentecost), and the Feast of Tabernacles. You can read about them in Leviticus 23 and Deuteronomy 16. These were opportunities for all of the people to have some holiday, since they were told not to work (in addition to the regular weekly Sabbath day, of course). But more than that, they were told to rejoice. "Rejoice before the Lord your God at the place he will choose as a dwelling for his Name" and "Be joyful at your festival" (Deut 16:11, 14). God's overflowing blessing each year should produce overflowing joy—with celebration, eating, drinking, and rejoicing.

The Old Testament has no embarrassment about celebrating the good gifts of God. Whatever God gives is to be received with thanksgiving and joy. That could include: the gift of the law; the annual gift of harvests; the word of God through the prophets; the building of the temple; a new king; and all the ordinary gifts of everyday life, such as work, love, marriage, beauty, nature, bread, and wine. There is so much to give thanks for, so much to give us joy. I wonder if, as Christians, we sometimes become so spiritual that we forget to take real pleasure in the ordinary gifts of God and don't allow ourselves to be filled to overflowing with joy.

However, having affirmed that point very strongly, we should notice that in the Old Testament the earthly joy of feasting together as an act of joyful thanks to God is protected and purified in two ways.

Joy must be morally clean. God warned Israel not to be tempted by the kind of debauched "joy" of the Canaanite festivals, which included sexual immorality, drunkenness, gluttony, and idolatry. They had two terrible object lessons about where that kind of sinful "joy" could lead. First, there was the wild orgy that happened at the foot of Mount Sinai while Moses was on the mountain receiving the Ten Commandments (recorded in Ex 32–34). And the second was in Moab, when they were tempted into immorality at Baal Peor on the advice of the pagan seer Balaam (Num 25; 31:16). By contrast with such sinful excess, Israel's feasts were to be full of fun and food, but not full of drunken immorality. They were to be occasions that the whole family could enjoy together without embarrassment (Deut 16:14).

Are we able to celebrate our joy as Christians like that? We will, if we follow the example of Jesus himself, who was able to enjoy a good party, a wedding banquet, and eating with his friends (including many people that nobody else would eat with). "The Son of Man came eating and drinking," he once said, when people contrasted him with John the Baptist and criticized him for eating with tax collectors, prostitutes, and sinners (Mt 11:19). Jesus could enjoy a good feast of food and drink without condoning sin and immorality.

And that is the message of the rest of the New Testament too. The Bible does not forbid drinking wine, but it does forbid drunkenness (1 Cor 5:11; Gal 5:21; Eph 5:18; 1 Pet 4:3). It does not forbid enjoying our food, but it does condemn gluttony (Prov 23:20-21; Titus 1:12). It does not forbid humor and laughter, but it does forbid "obscenity, foolish talk or coarse joking" (Eph 5:4)—the sort that is filthy or hurtful to others. The Bible gives us abundant room and reasons for joy, but warns us against letting celebration sink into degradation.

Joy must be socially inclusive. God commanded the Israelites to have their festivals, to take time off, to have great parties with lots of food and drink—but he also told them to make sure that nobody got left out. This is emphasized twice in Deuteronomy's instructions for the festivals.

And rejoice before the LORD your God at the place he will
choose as a dwelling for his Name—you, your sons and daughters,
*your male and female servants, the Levites in your towns, and the
foreigners, the fatherless and the widows living among you.* (Deut
16:11, repeated at v. 14, emphasis mine)

In other words, Israelite family members were not to enjoy a big feast
while all the servants did the hard work. And they were to take particular care to include those who did not have *land* of their own to
harvest (Levites and foreigners), and to include those who did not
have *families* to provide for them (orphans and widows).

One concrete example of this principle in action is found in Nehemiah 8. The people of Israel had returned from exile to Judah. Nehemiah had led them in rebuilding the wall around Jerusalem. Then
he led them in a great occasion of covenant renewal. As part of that,
Ezra read the law aloud to the people and the Levites translated and
explained it to them so they could all understand it. When the people
began to weep (probably because of conviction of their sin and failure),
Nehemiah and Ezra encouraged them not to weep, but to rejoice on
this great occasion of returning to the Lord and his covenant. Nehemiah told the people to go and enjoy party food and celebrate! But,
he added, make sure you provide for those who don't have any food
and drink of their own. Nobody should be left out. "Nehemiah said,
'Go and enjoy choice food and sweet drinks, and send some to those
who have nothing prepared. This day is holy to our Lord. Do not
grieve, for the joy of the LORD is your strength'" (Neh 8:10).

Jesus made the same point to his disciples. In fact, he made it while
at a meal, and he probably embarrassed his host when he said this. He
warned them not to have a party for their close friends and neighbors
only, but also to invite those who usually didn't get such invitations—
the poor, needy, and disabled (Lk 14:12-14). I have to confess that I
think this is one of the clearest commands of Jesus that many of us
regularly ignore. I feel convicted of my own failure even as I write this.

It is a sad fact that festivals like Christmas and Thanksgiving can be among the loneliest times of year for those who are elderly, or strangers in a community, or those living on their own without families, or those who are literally homeless.

So the joy that is the fruit of the Spirit, if we think of it in the light of the Bible, can include the sheer joy of eating and drinking together. Joy is a feast. No wonder Jesus used that picture to describe the future that we will enjoy with him in the new creation, in the messianic banquet. But our feasting needs to reflect the joy of the *Holy* Spirit, and so it will be clean and wholesome and not tainted with immorality, greed, gluttony, or excess. And it will be inclusive, making sure that all those who belong to the family of God are included, and not just those we happen to like.

Joy Is Having a Faith

The word *gospel*, as I'm sure you know, simply means "good news." And *good* news brings joy just by being what it is—good! So if the biblical gospel is the best and greatest good news the world has ever heard, then there is no greater joy than knowing and believing the gospel.

The gospel tells us the great truths of what God has done through Christ to save the world, because of his love and grace. In the gospel, God promises us forgiveness, eternal life, and a future filled with hope for the whole creation. And these are things that can never be taken away, because they are rooted in who God is and what God has done. And they are simply brimming over with joy! How can we not be glad when we know the good news and believe it?

We could take a lot of time at this point just enjoying the vast scope of the biblical gospel and thanking God that by his grace we have come to put our faith in Christ. That's because the gospel is not just a formula or a mechanism to get to heaven, but is the good news of the whole Bible story of all that God promised and accomplished through Christ. Even a summary of it should bring us joy, as for example, from a statement known as *The Cape Town Commitment: A Confession of Faith and a Call to Action* from the Third Lausanne Congress on World Evangelization, in Cape Town, South Africa, in October 2010:

> *We love the story the gospel tells.* The gospel announces as good news the historical events of the life, death and resurrection of Jesus of Nazareth. As the son of David, the promised Messiah King, Jesus is the one through whom alone God established his kingdom and acted for the salvation of the world, enabling all nations on earth to be blessed, as he promised Abraham. Paul defines the gospel in stating that "Christ died for our sins according to the scriptures, that he was buried, that he was raised on the third day, according to the scriptures, and that he appeared to Peter and then to the Twelve." The gospel declares that, on the cross of Christ, God took upon himself, in the person of his Son and in our place, the judgment our sin deserves. In the same great saving act, completed, vindicated and declared through the resurrection, God won the decisive victory over Satan, death and all evil powers, liberated us from their power and fear, and ensured their eventual destruction. God accomplished the reconciliation of believers with himself and with one another across all boundaries and enmities. God also accomplished his purpose of the ultimate reconciliation of all creation, and in the bodily resurrection of Jesus has given us the first fruits of the new creation. "God was in Christ reconciling the world to himself." How we love the gospel story!
>
> *We love the assurance the gospel brings.* Solely through trusting in Christ alone, we are united with Christ through the Holy Spirit and are counted righteous in Christ before God. Being justified by faith we have peace with God and no longer face condemnation. We receive the forgiveness of our sins. We are born again into a living hope by sharing Christ's risen life. We

are adopted as fellow heirs with Christ. We become citizens of God's covenant people, members of God's family and the place of God's dwelling. So by trusting in Christ, we have full assurance of salvation and eternal life, for our salvation ultimately depends, not on ourselves, but on the work of Christ and the promise of God. "Nothing in all creation will be able to separate us from the love of God that is in Christ Jesus our Lord." How we love the gospel's promise!

The joy that is generated by our faith in these great truths and promises can be present in our lives, even when there is suffering, loss, bereavement, illness, or accident, and even in situations of persecution and martyrdom. Such things, whether trivial or terrible, cannot and do not take away the inner joy that is the fruit of the Spirit.

In the Old Testament, the book of Psalms is called, in Hebrew, "The Praises." And yet the single largest category of "praises" within it consists of laments! That is, people were bringing before God their personal pain, their experience of injustice or oppression, physical or verbal attacks, life-threatening illness, etc. Their songs are totally honest about these things. They did not pretend that everything was fine and try to look happy anyway (the way we may feel pressured to do in church). And yet, by bringing all their suffering into the presence of God, they were able to turn back to hope, praise, and even joy, because of their unshakeable faith that God was sovereign and would never abandon them. That kind of joy can cope with the pain, because it is the fruit of faith in the living God.

Think of Habakkuk. His country was facing a devastating invasion that might destroy everything. He was trembling with fear at the prospect (Hab 3:16). But even in such circumstances he knew he could trust in God and rejoice in him—with this remarkable affirmation of faith:

Though the fig tree does not bud
and there are no grapes on the vines,

> though the olive crop fails
>   and the fields produce no food,
> though there are no sheep in the pen
>   and no cattle in the stalls,
> yet I will rejoice in the Lord,
>   I will be joyful in God my Savior. (Hab 3:17-18)

Jesus told his disciples to rejoice when they were persecuted—an astonishing command, but when the time came, they actually did (Mt 5:11-12; Acts 5:40-41).

Then think of the apostle Paul. Some of the times when Paul wrote most enthusiastically about joy in his letters were when he himself was chained up in a stinking Roman prison, sometimes after a flogging. He would have been cold, hungry, weak, and in great pain. Yet he had the joy of the gospel of Christ within him. One time, he and Silas were singing psalms in such circumstances (Acts 16:25)! Even in terrible personal suffering, Paul could rejoice in the gospel, and tell others to do the same. And when Peter wrote to Christians who were already suffering a lot under persecution, his opening chapter rang with "inexpressible and glorious joy" (1 Pet 1:6-9). So, in the New Testament, the joy that is the fruit of the Spirit, the joy that comes from having faith in the gospel, is a strong, robust joy that is not wiped out by suffering.

Now at this point, we do need to be careful. We need to distinguish between, on the one hand, Christians who are suffering the ordinary struggles of life and may need some encouragement to hold on to their joy in the midst of their troubles, and, on the other hand, Christians who are suffering the illness of clinical depression. Depression can be a real and devastating illness and there are physical and psychological causes that need wise and professional medical care, just as for any other illness. So if we have a Christian sister or brother who is suffering from that kind of medically diagnosed depression, we should not come along with a happy greeting, telling them to "cheer up, snap out of it, and be joyful in the Lord." That can be very insensitive, and indeed it may add to their suffering, for "being joyful in the Lord" is exactly what they long to do, but can't. Loss of joy in life is one of the worst symptoms of depressive illness. And getting joy back is not just a matter of "trying harder." Depression is an illness, not a failure or a weakness.

And yet, at the same time, I know a number of Christians who suffer from depression, including within my family, and they testify to the fact that they still have their underlying assurance of the truth of the gospel and the love of God. They know that God can be trusted, even when life is at its darkest. And knowing those things deep down means that they can know joy as an objective *fact or truth*, even when they don't have joyful emotional *feelings*. Poet and hymnodist William Cowper suffered terribly from depressive illness, and it was out of that experience that he could write lines such as,

> Judge not the Lord by feeble sense,
> But trust him for his grace.
> Behind a frowning Providence,
> He hides a smiling face.

That's why joy, Christian joy as the fruit of the Spirit, is not just an *emotion*, but flows from the exercise, in our minds and wills, of faith in God's promises in Christ.

Joy Is Having a Future

The fourth thing I mentioned that brings me joy is being out enjoying God's creation. And of course we can and should celebrate creation with joy! The Old Testament psalmists did it with great energy and beauty, as for example in Psalms 65 and 104. But the Bible doesn't only talk about human beings rejoicing in creation. It tells us that the whole of creation itself rejoices and praises God. I don't know how this happens, or how God receives such joy and praise from the non-human creation—but the Bible says that he does.

But at the same time, we know that creation in its present state is not how it will fully become by God's power. The earth is cursed because of our sin—though one day that will be removed (Rev 22:3). And the whole of creation is frustrated in its purpose of bringing praise and glory to God (Rom 8:20). But not forever! The Bible tells us that God's plan of redemption includes the whole creation. It is not that we will some day be saved *out of* the earth, but that we will be saved *along with* the whole creation. That is the combined message of Romans 8:16-24.

This is a biblical truth that goes back to the Old Testament also. Isaiah tells us that God is already busy creating a new heaven and a new earth, and the way he portrays it is filled with wonder, joy, satisfaction, and safety (Is 65:17-25). In the light of that great hope, some psalms look forward to the whole creation rejoicing together, when God comes to put things right.

> Let the heavens rejoice, let the earth be glad;
>> let the sea resound, and all that is in it.
> Let the fields be jubilant, and everything in them;
>> let all the trees of the forest sing for joy.
> Let all creation rejoice before the Lord, for he comes,
>> he comes to judge the earth.
> He will judge the world in righteousness
>> and the peoples in his faithfulness. (Ps 96:11-13)

Psalm 98 ends the same way, but adds the rivers and mountains, clapping and singing for joy!

Paul tells us, in that amazing survey of the glory of the Lord Jesus Christ, God's Son, that the whole of creation ("all things in heaven and earth") have been created by him, are sustained by him, and have been reconciled to God by him through the blood of his cross (Col 1:15-20).

The joy of creation is Christ-centered from beginning to end, and the means by which we are saved (the cross of Christ) is the means by which also creation will be restored. Surely that multiplies our joy by the number of grains of sand on the shore and stars in the sky!

And the Bible ends, not with us going up and away to some other destination, but with God coming down to dwell with redeemed humanity in the new creation (Rev 21:1-5). And with that prospect, John tells us that in his vision,

> Then I heard every creature in heaven and on earth and under the earth and on the sea, and all that is in them, saying:
>
> "To him who sits on the throne and to the Lamb
> be praise and honor and glory and power,
> for ever and ever!" (Rev 5:13)

So then, since we are destined to share the joy of creation, and since creation is destined to share in our joy (when both we and it are finally redeemed by God's grace), then we can experience that joy now as we anticipate it. Joy is filled with hope for a wonderful future for the whole creation, including ourselves.

A Final Thought

If joy is an essential feature of the life of Christians who are filled with God's Spirit and bearing the fruit of the Spirit, *why then is it so often missing in our lives?* Why are Christians so miserable so often?

Maybe because we simply *forget.* It's easy to get tired and irritable and then to fall into self-pity. And self-pity is the great enemy of joy. We need to make ourselves remember the great truths of the gospel from the Bible itself. We need to go over them in our minds until we realize how inconsistent it is to say we *believe* such wonderful gospel truths, and then still go around filled with misery and feeling sorry for ourselves and spreading gloom on all those around us. Speaking personally, I find that I need to speak severely to myself along those lines quite often, for I am easily tempted to feel down and sorry for myself. Then I repent, remind myself of the gospel of

God's grace, and pray for the joy of the Spirit to bear fruit in my life and thinking.

Or maybe it's because we are suspicious of joy. Life is a serious business, we may say. And so it is. We may think that Christianity is more than just having a laugh. And so it is. But that doesn't mean we should not have hearts that are filled with joy when our lives are filled with the Holy Spirit. After all, the Bible shows us very clearly that God not only *wants* us to be joyful, but actually *commands* us to be! It sounds strange to say that "joy is a duty," but it is a happy duty! Paul was happy to repeat the command, so let's obey it! "Rejoice in the Lord always. I will say it again: Rejoice!" (Phil 4:4).

Questions

1. What are the main reasons for great celebrations of joy in your culture? Can Christians enter into them, or are they contrary to the Bible's teaching? In what ways?

2. Has the gospel transformed any of your culture's festivals into occasions for Christian joy?

3. Is there a difference between joy as the fruit of the Spirit and ordinary cheerfulness and happiness? If so, what makes that difference?

4. Do you know of examples of people (including possibly yourself) who have suffered greatly and yet still showed joy in their faith—even if they died for it?

Watch a video from Chris about joy
at **ivpress.com/cultivating-joy**.

3

PEACE

"Go away and give me peace!"

"Let's have some peace around here!"

Familiar cries of frustration in the hurly-burly of life! There is not much peace for many of us, it seems. There are demanding families to manage, or stresses and pressures at work to endure. There are strained relationships to cope with, or perhaps even abusive ones. There are anxieties about life—in the immediate or long-term future. And all the time, the bustle and busyness of life swirls around, multiplied for many people by the seemingly inescapable invasion of the Internet, emails, social media, etc.

Peace? If only . . .

Yet peace is one of those huge words in the Bible. In the Old Testament it is that beautiful and complex word *shalom*—all-round well-being, freedom from fear and want, and contentment in relationship with God, others, and creation. Peace in the storm is God's gift to his people (Ps 29:11). Peace is God's promise—when love, justice, truth, and peace have a group hug, and heaven and earth are in harmony (Ps 85:8-10). Jesus and Paul would have used the word *peace* many times every day in their customary greetings to other Jews ("Peace be with you"), as is still the case among Jews and Arabs today. It is a rich, resonant, and profoundly meaningful word.

But when Paul gives peace third place in the fruit of the Spirit, what does he have in mind? Well, he talks about peace a lot in his letters, and we can distinguish several ways in which he uses the word. Not all of them are quite what he includes in the fruit of the Spirit, but it is still useful to see the different dimensions of the word and then zoom in on those dimensions that Paul expects to see growing like fruit in our lives.

The Peace That God Made

At times Paul talks about peace as something that God, and only God, has accomplished. That means the peace that is the result of the great work of atonement that God accomplished through Jesus Christ in his cross and resurrection. One of the clearest explanations of this is in Ephesians 2. I have put the peace phrases in italics.

> Therefore, remember that formerly you who are Gentiles by birth and called "uncircumcised" by those who call themselves "the circumcision" (which is done in the body by human hands)— remember that at that time you were separate from Christ, excluded from citizenship in Israel and foreigners to the covenants of the promise, without hope and without God in the world. But now in Christ Jesus you who once were far away have been brought near by the blood of Christ.
>
> For *he himself is our peace,* who has made the two groups one and has destroyed the barrier, the dividing wall of hostility, by setting aside in his flesh the law with its commands and regulations. His purpose was to create in himself one new humanity out of the two, *thus making peace,* and in one body to reconcile both of them to God through the cross, by which he put to death their hostility. He came and *preached peace* to you who were far away and peace to those who were near. For through him we both have access to the Father by one Spirit. (Eph 2:11-18, emphasis mine)

Notice how Paul uses peace three times. First, Christ "is our peace"—that is, whatever peace we have as reconciled enemies, we have in Christ. And that can only be true because, second, he "made peace" by abolishing, through the cross, the barrier of enmity that divided Gentiles and Jews. And then, third, through the preaching of the apostles, Christ came and "preached peace" to those who had once been far away.

So in this context, Paul is talking about the "once-for-all" peace achieved by God's work though Christ at the cross. It's something that God did for us. It's not the peace that is the fruit of the Spirit in our lives. Peace as the fruit of the Spirit has to do with our character here and now, rather than God's action back then. So, although this aspect of peace—the peace that God made—is absolutely fundamental to the gospel, it is probably not what Paul means by peace as the fruit of the Spirit in Galatians 5.

The Peace That God Gives

Perhaps, then, Paul had in mind *the peace that God gives*. And that comes in two dimensions. There is peace *with* God, and there is the peace *of* God.

Peace with God. This is the much-loved statement of Paul at the start of Romans 5: "Therefore, since we have been justified through faith, we have *peace with God* through our Lord Jesus Christ, through whom we have gained access by faith into this grace in which we now stand" (Rom 5:1-2, emphasis mine).

When we put our trust in Jesus, who died for our sins, then we know that we come into a right relationship with God, which gives us peace. Peace with God means peace of heart and conscience, the absence of guilt and fear. We no longer need to be anxious about God's verdict on the last day. In Christ we are declared to be among the righteous, those who belong to God's family. And it is all because of God's grace. That is a wonderful thing and is perhaps a bit closer to the meaning of peace as the fruit of the Spirit. For unless we are at peace with God through faith, the Spirit of God is not at work in our lives. But once our relationship with God is settled, then the Spirit of God pours his new life into our lives and that life of God begins to bear fruit.

The peace of God. But the peace that God gives is not only peace *with God,* but also the peace *of God.* That means peace of mind, freedom from anxiety and panic. Jesus told us not to be worried but to trust our Heavenly Father. His words describe a quality of peace that reflects the presence of God's Spirit:

> Therefore I tell you, do not worry about your life, what you will eat or drink; or about your body, what you will wear. Is not life more than food, and the body more than clothes? Look at the birds of the air; they do not sow or reap or store away in barns, and yet your heavenly Father feeds them. Are you not much more valuable than they? Can any one of you by worrying add a single hour to your life?
>
> And why do you worry about clothes? See how the flowers of the field grow. They do not labor or spin. Yet I tell you that not even Solomon in all his splendor was dressed like one of these. If that is how God clothes the grass of the field, which is here today and tomorrow is thrown into the fire, will he not much more clothe you—you of little faith? So do not worry, saying, "What shall we eat?" or "What shall we drink?" or "What shall we wear?" For the pagans run after all these things, and your heavenly Father knows that you need them. But seek first his kingdom and his righteousness, and all these things will be given to you as well. Therefore do not worry about tomorrow, for tomorrow will worry about itself. Each day has enough trouble of its own. (Mt 6:25-34)

Paul echoes Jesus' teaching, and explicitly links it to the peace that God gives: "Do not be anxious about anything, but in every situation, by prayer and petition, with thanksgiving, present your requests to God. And the peace of God, which transcends all understanding, will guard your hearts and minds in Christ Jesus" (Phil 4:6-7).

This is not just a blasé, "happy-go-lucky" attitude. Rather it is a settled trust in God's Fatherly care and a steady refusal to give in to anxieties. It is an act of will, in which we *choose* not to worry, but to pray and trust God. And the whole Bible assures us that God can be trusted. Be at peace.

But, back in the so-called real world—the world of daily work and busyness—can we have peace there? Can we have peace in the midst of all the stresses of life here and now, in the workplace or home? Not only would Paul answer, "Yes we can," but also I think he would add that *that is exactly where it matters most.* For a life that is filled with this kind of peace is a powerful witness to the gospel. It is in the non-Christian home or workplace that the people who live with the peace of God in their hearts, and who work to create or restore peace among others, stand out and get noticed.

Joy and peace go together, as we mentioned in the last chapter. Christians will be noticed (and often asked questions) if they have the kind of joy that is not affected by the moods of cynical despair and negativity that can easily dominate groups of people thrown together by their work. But equally, their joy doesn't come from getting swept up in occasional crazy bouts of drinking and gluttony. Rather they have a quality of inner joy that can be sensed even in times of pain, or loss, or suffering; an underlying joy that is not dependent on alcohol, sex, or money.

Similarly, Christians with peace, who are not racked by anxiety or driven by ruthless ambition, who are not devastated by failing to get promoted, or in despair because of the threat or reality of losing their job, but who rather have an inner peace that flows from trusting God—such people are bearing silent witness to the Lord Jesus Christ. They are being like Christ in trusting their heavenly Father in the midst of whatever life brings—even the tough things.

Cultivating the fruit of the Spirit, you see, is not about polishing your own halo, or keeping up a good image. That sort of thing is stupid and false, and everybody (including God) can see through it. It's about making Christ visible and making the gospel attractive.

The peace that God calls for. We have thought about the peace God made (through the cross of Christ) and the peace God gives (peace of mind and conscience). But there is a third kind of peace, and that is *the peace that God calls us to work at in the way we live.* God calls us to *live at peace* with others, and to *work for peace* among Christians—and indeed in the wider world. This is by far the most frequent way that Paul uses the word, and it's almost certainly the kind of peace he particularly has in mind in his list of the fruit of the Spirit in Galatians 5:22-23.

Since God has made peace between himself and us (at his own great cost through the death of Jesus on the cross), God now calls us to live in peace with one another, as a way of "living out" the transforming power of the cross in our own practical lives. But that does not come naturally to us in our fallen sinfulness and dividedness. It is something that has to be cultivated like fruit—the fruit of God's Spirit at work within us and between us. That's why Paul can both describe it as fruit and also tell us to "make every effort" to live in that way.

One of the best places to think through what this means would be to go back to that text where we found joy and peace closely linked—Romans 14:1–15:13. Paul was writing to the Christians in the great cosmopolitan city of Rome. Many of them had come to faith from a completely pagan, Gentile background. They had no qualms about any kind of food or particular holy days. But some of the Christians in Rome were Jews who had now come to faith in Jesus as Messiah. There were enormous differences between these groups, even though they were all now believers in Jesus and together in the church. They came from very different cultures and religious backgrounds. Some thought they could eat any meat from the butcher's shop, as they had always done. Others were horrified because they thought that kind of meat was unclean and idolatrous. Some wanted to observe the Sabbath day as they had always done. Others didn't care what day it was; they had to work every day anyway (especially if they were slaves), so what difference would a Sabbath make?

It seems that those from a Gentile background were thinking of themselves as "the strong" (i.e. they had a strong faith and knew that things like food and days didn't affect their salvation and relationship with Christ). And maybe they were calling the Jewish believers "the weak" because they were still attached to their Jewish customs and scruples, only eating vegetables, for example, to avoid any contamination from meat that was ritually unclean or sacrificed to idols.

Now these were not minor things. We might think, "What a fuss about meat or vegetables! Why did it matter?" But it did matter a lot to them—especially the Jewish believers. These differences of cultural and religious background were causing a lot of disagreement and dispute, theologically and practically. But Paul spends a chapter and a half urging both sides to "accept one another" and to avoid quarrelling over "disputable matters." Notice that Paul takes it for granted that there are always going to be "disputable matters" in any group of Christians. We will not always agree about everything. Such is life. But the key thing is not that we should *agree* with one another all the time, but that we should *accept* one another—even those who see things very differently—when we know that the other person is a believer and loves the Lord Jesus Christ as we do. Here's how Paul begins:

> Accept the one whose faith is weak, without quarreling over disputable matters. One person's faith allows them to eat anything, but another, whose faith is weak, eats only vegetables. The one who eats everything must not treat with contempt the one who does not, and the one who does not eat everything must not judge the one who does, for God has accepted them. (Rom 14:1-3)

Paul starts by telling them categorically that they must avoid two opposite attitudes that can very easily poison any Christian church. So he tells them in verse 3, *no contempt!* That is, Gentile Christians must not mock Jewish believers for what seemed to be out-of-date rules and scruples about food and days; and *No condemnation!* That is, Jewish believers must not denounce Gentiles for what seemed (to Jews) to be much too free and easy behavior.

Rather, Paul commands them to "make every effort to do what leads to peace" (Rom 14:19). That is his fundamental instruction in this whole section. And he reinforces it with a whole range of arguments that we should take very seriously.

We are subject to the same Lord (Rom 14:1-12). This is the main thrust of the first part of Paul's case, and it has several aspects:

- We have been accepted by the same Lord (Rom 14:3; 15:7). Whatever our opinions on various matters, we have been accepted by God, in Christ. In fact, the very heart of the gospel is that God has not only accepted both Jews and Gentiles in Christ, but also he has made them into one new humanity, as Paul explains in Ephesians 2. So we share the same gospel too, and that gospel has made us one. So if I reject, or refuse to meet with, or denounce, another person who is a believer in Jesus as Lord and Savior, then effectively I am saying to that person, "Well, God may have accepted you, but I don't. Christ has welcomed you, but I don't." That is a serious sin against the gospel itself.

- We are all servants of the same Master, so we have no right to judge one another (Rom 14:4). Only God (our Master) has the right to judge each of us—and he will. So don't assume a posture of judgment that belongs only to God.

- We all live "to the Lord"—in all of life, and indeed in life or death (Rom 14:5-9). Whatever we do, then, needs to be done as in *his* presence, subject to *his* approval, not in order to please others.

- We are ultimately all accountable to God alone as Judge (Rom 14:10-12). And when we look forward to that day of judgment, our differences here and now should begin to look much less significant. When we stand before the judgment seat of God, what difference will it make then that I was an enthusiastic charismatic and you stuck seriously to very sober worship? What difference will it make that I was a Brazilian Pentecostal and you were a western Anglican? What difference will it make that I thought the millennium should have come first, but you thought it had already happened? What difference will it make that I was an African woman who preached the gospel, planted churches, and taught thousands of people how to be disciples, but you thought I shouldn't have been doing that at all as a woman? And if things like that will not matter *then*, at the judgment seat of Christ, why do we let them matter so much *now* that they divide us into warring camps?

We are constrained by love (Rom 14:13-23). What Paul writes here is very similar to his teaching in 1 Corinthians 8 and 10 about meat that had been sacrificed to idols. Paul says that Christians have freedom in what they eat or drink, because all food ultimately comes from God and can be received with thanksgiving. But to flaunt your freedom over other Christians, without any sensitivity for their conscientious feelings in the matter, is to fail to exercise Christian love—and that is a serious sin. For in fact, when you sin against another believer, you sin against Christ (1 Cor 8:12).

Paul is not saying that everybody must just conform to the person with the most scruples. That can become very manipulative in a Christian fellowship. Everybody defers to the weakest, and the weakest thus paradoxically exercises huge power! What Paul says in Romans 14:14 assumes that there is a place for helping people to come to a more mature understanding of what being a Christian means, and what it doesn't mean. All of us need to educate our consciences through ongoing study of the Scriptures, prayer, and fellowship. That will help us get a better balance between where we can act with maturity and freedom, and where we need to exercise loving restraint and sensitivity. And that is never easy! We often think or say, "Where should I draw the line?" There is no easy answer to that. But let us not be so obsessed with drawing lines that we end up dividing the body of Christ and forgetting the mission we should be doing for him. The love we live by is more important than the lines we draw.

We are to be shaped by the example of Christ (Rom 15:1-8). Paul comes to the climax of his argument by focusing our eyes again on Jesus Christ himself. What he says in Romans 15:2 is very similar to Philippians 2:

> Do nothing out of selfish ambition or vain conceit. Rather, in humility value others above yourselves, not looking to your own interests but each of you to the interests of the others. In your relationships with one another, have the same mindset as Christ Jesus. (Phil 2:3-5)

And in both places, he makes Jesus the example of what he instructs us to do: "For even Christ did not please himself but, as it is written: 'The insults of those who insult you have fallen on me'" (Rom 15:3).

That quotation comes from Psalm 69, which is a picture of unjust suffering. But whereas the psalmist there called out for God's judgment on those who were tormenting him (Ps 69:7-8), Jesus prayed that his Father would forgive those who were crucifying him. And Paul tells us to follow his example—as Stephen, the first martyr for Jesus, did (Acts 7:59-60). So in Romans 15 verses 4 and 13, Paul connects the example of Jesus to the Scriptures, and makes that part of the recipe for being filled with hope, peace, and joy.

But Paul goes even further and turns his teaching into a very powerful prayer: "May the God who gives endurance and encouragement give you the same attitude of mind toward each other that Christ Jesus had, so that with one mind and one voice you may glorify the God and Father of our Lord Jesus Christ" (Rom 15:5-6).

Paul shows us what true peace among believers means (when they accept one another and work hard to live at peace with others, even when they disagree). It means that they have the mind of Christ. It means they can truly sing together with one voice in their worship. And it means that they will bring glory to God the Father. That all sounds wonderful. But when you think of the opposite in each case, it is a strong warning.

When we fight and condemn one another, denounce other Christians and divide from them, fostering all kinds of divisions within the church, then we do not have the mind of Christ. We make a mockery of singing "with one voice" in our worship and deprive God of his glory.

Peace, as Paul describes it, is a serious business. It is not just a nice happy feeling. It is at the heart of the gospel of Christ and the glory of God. Surely Paul would say all this just as sternly to churches today, where we find seemingly endless condemnation of other Christians who see things differently from ourselves. Would he not add, as he did to the Galatians, "If you bite and devour each other, watch out or you will be destroyed by each other" (Gal 5:15)?

For Paul, seeking peace and living at peace is a very important part of living together as Christians. And in case you think I have spent too much time on that section in Romans 14–15, it is only because that is where Paul expands and explains it so thoroughly. But just look at how many other times he says the same thing more briefly:

- "If it is possible, as far as it depends on you, live at peace with everyone" (Rom 12:18).
- "God has called us to live in peace" (1 Cor 7:15, in the context of marriage).
- "God is not a God of disorder but of peace" (1 Cor 14:33, in the context of our services of worship).

- "Strive for full restoration, encourage one another, be of one mind, live in peace. And the God of love and peace will be with you" (2 Cor 13:11, in the context of church divisions).

- "Make every effort to keep the unity of the Spirit through the bond of peace" (Eph 4:3).

- "Let the peace of Christ rule in your hearts, since as members of one body you were called to peace" (Col 3:15).

What does it mean to practice peace like that—to cultivate that fruit of the Spirit in our lives?

Well, at the very least it should mean that we do the following:

- We should seek to address and resolve conflicts among ourselves, rather than adding to them (or causing them in the first place).

- We should be careful to avoid the kind of words and attitudes that easily create misunderstanding and division.

- We should be quick to apologize and say sorry, even if we were not, strictly speaking, the ones in the wrong! "Sorry" may be the hardest word, but it is often the first one that leads back to peace.

- We shouldn't jump to defend ourselves when things are said or done against us, but allow God to vindicate the truth in his own time. Paul said it is better to suffer wrong than to take other Christians to court.

- We need to follow carefully the instructions of Jesus on how brothers and sisters should deal with grievances against one another (Mt 18:15-17), rather than just going public in the press or on blogs, etc., about other people.

- Above all, we should avoid all kinds of gossip about others, and learn the strict discipline of keeping confidences.

Perhaps the best way to end this chapter would be with the prayer commonly attributed to St. Francis of Assisi (though strictly speaking the author is unknown).

Lord, make me an instrument of thy peace;
    where there is hatred, let me sow love;
    where there is injury, pardon;
    where there is doubt, faith;
    where there is despair, hope;
    where there is darkness, light;
    and where there is sadness, joy.

O Divine Master,
    grant that I may not so much seek to be consoled
        as to console;
    to be understood, as to understand;
    to be loved, as to love.
For it is in giving that we receive,
    it is in pardoning that we are pardoned,
    and it is in dying that we are born to eternal life.
Amen.

Questions

1. What Bible stories illustrate the power of reconciliation and peacemaking?

2. What examples can you think of within your own church or culture where Christians have been instrumental in bringing peace and reconciliation?

3. Are there conflicts and divisions at present within your church or wider Christian community? Consider studying Romans 14–15 together as a way of working toward building peace and reconciliation.

4. In what ways do you think your own life displays peace as the fruit of the Spirit, and in what ways do you need to pray for this to be more true than it is now?

Watch a video from Chris about peace at
ivpress.com/cultivating-peace.

4

PATIENCE

Love, joy, peace.

The first three items in Paul's fruit basket sound very spiritual. Heavenly almost. Very nice for Sundays, at least. But his next one, patience, brings us back down to earth on a Monday. What are we like to live with the rest of the week? How do we cope with all that presses in on us in the hustle and hassle of life?

The word Paul uses literally means "long-tempered." In our older English translations patience was translated "long-suffering"—one of those old-fashioned words that really deserves to be kept alive. More recently, it is translated "forbearance." Actually both meanings are needed to get the full flavor of Paul's term. Patience as fruit of the Spirit means:

- The ability to endure for a long time whatever opposition and suffering may come our way, and to show perseverance without wanting retaliation or revenge.

- The ability to put up with the weaknesses and foibles of others (including other believers), and to show forbearance toward them, without getting quickly irritated or angry enough to want to fight back.

So patience is a tough sort of word. It demands strength and stamina, and it depends on being able to exercise control over our reactions to others. None of that is easy. It doesn't come naturally to us, which is why we need the Spirit of God to make it grow in our lives.

But before we think about how *we* should behave, we should start by thinking about the patience of God himself. Remember, when we talk about the fruit of the Spirit, it means that God's own character is bearing fruit in our character. The life of God is at work within our life.

The Patience of God in the Old Testament

Maybe you wouldn't think of the patience of God in the Old Testament. Many people think that the so-called Old Testament God was always angry, or suddenly angry. Well, there are certainly some spectacular examples of God's anger against people's sin or presumption. But in fact when God identified and described himself to Moses, this is what he said: "The LORD, the LORD, the compassionate and gracious God, slow to anger, abounding in love and faithfulness" (Ex 34:6).

"Slow to anger" is a good way of expressing what we mean by patience. Now, that definitive statement comes in the context of a great sin by the people of Israel at Mount Sinai. It was their apostasy and idolatry with the golden calf (Ex 32). And certainly God did exercise judgment on that occasion. But whereas he had threatened to destroy them completely, God's response to Moses' intercession was to spare the nation as a whole and continue to lead them forward (Ex 33:12-17).

That famous verse (Ex 34:6) is echoed quite often in the Old Testament. One of the most beautiful examples is in Psalm 103:

> The LORD is compassionate and gracious,
>> slow to anger, abounding in love.

He will not always accuse,
    nor will he harbor his anger forever;
he does not treat us as our sins deserve
    or repay us according to our iniquities. (Ps 103:8-10)

A little later the psalmist compares God's compassion to the way a father responds to his children—which certainly takes a lot of patience!

Even when judgment is clearly deserved, God is patient, especially when there is a chance of repentance. That's what Jonah discovered. Well, actually Jonah knew it already, and so he criticizes God for being so patient and forgiving! Jonah was embarrassed and angry by the very quality that God had so often shown to Israel, when it was for the benefit of hated foreigners (Jon 3:10–4:4).

"Slow to anger," said God about himself. And even when God's anger is rightly and necessarily aroused by human wickedness and sin, his anger does not last forever. Micah saw that aspect of God's character (that he does not stay angry forever) as something unique about Yahweh the God of Israel, something that was not true of other alleged gods.

Who is a God like you,
    who pardons sin and forgives the transgression
    of the remnant of his inheritance?
You do not stay angry forever
    but delight to show mercy.
You will again have compassion on us;
    you will tread our sins underfoot
    and hurl all our iniquities into the depths of the sea.
      (Mic 7:18-19)

In the history of Israel in the Old Testament, yes there were times of God's anger, but they need to be seen in the light of the long story of God's patience over many centuries and generations. Often, God's judgment fell only after many years of warnings and appeals through prophet after prophet. In fact, some of those prophets themselves marveled at the patience of God in the face of Israel's constant rebellion and sin. Below are a few examples.

Hosea. God had been as patient with Israel as parents have to be with children who keep going astray. Parental patience is beautifully expressed in God's words through Hosea.

> When Israel was a child, I loved him,
> > and out of Egypt I called my son.
> But the more they were called,
> > the more they went away from me.
> They sacrificed to the Baals
> > and they burned incense to images.
> It was I who taught Ephraim to walk,
> > taking them by the arms;
> but they did not realize
> > it was I who healed them.
> I led them with cords of human kindness,
> > with ties of love.
> To them I was like one who lifts
> > a little child to the cheek,
> > and I bent down to feed them. (Hos 11:1-4)

Jeremiah. He spent forty years of his life pleading patiently with Israel to turn back to God and change their ways, but they wouldn't. This is how God speaks through Jeremiah:

> I myself said,
> "'How gladly would I treat you like my children
> > and give you a pleasant land,
> > the most beautiful inheritance of any nation.'
> I thought you would call me 'Father'
> > and not turn away from following me.

But like a woman unfaithful to her husband,
    so you, Israel, have been unfaithful to me,"
declares the LORD. (Jer 3:19-20)

Say to them, 'This is what the LORD says:

    "'When people fall down, do they not get up?
        When someone turns away, do they not return?
Why then have these people turned away?
    Why does Jerusalem always turn away?
They cling to deceit;
    they refuse to return.
I have listened attentively,
    but they do not say what is right.
None of them repent of their wickedness,
    saying, "What have I done?"
Each pursues their own course
    like a horse charging into battle.
Even the stork in the sky
    knows her appointed seasons,
and the dove, the swift and the thrush
    observe the time of their migration.
But my people do not know
    the requirements of the LORD. (Jer 8:4-7)

For twenty-three years—from the thirteenth year of Josiah son of Amon king of Judah until this very day—the word of the LORD has come to me and I have spoken to you again and again, but you have not listened.

And though the LORD has sent all his servants the prophets to you again and again, you have not listened or paid any attention. (Jer 25:3-4)

Perhaps it was Jeremiah especially, then, that James had in mind when he makes the prophets his prime example of patience. "Brothers and sisters, as an example of patience in the face of suffering, take the prophets who spoke in the name of the Lord" (Jas 5:10).

Patience has a lot to do with how much you are able to bear or carry. That's why, when we run out of patience, we say "I can't bear it anymore." Isaiah pictures an argument between God and Israel, in which God says that he had not laid a burden on them, but on the contrary, they had constantly wearied him with their sins.

> I have not burdened you with grain offerings
>> nor wearied you with demands for incense. . . .
> But you have burdened me with your sins
>> and wearied me with your offenses. (Is 43:23-24)

This does not mean, of course, that God literally gets tired. What it does mean is that when God is being patient it is because he is carrying the heavy load of human sin. Indeed, one of the Hebrew words that is translated "to forgive" literally means "to bear or carry." So when God is patient, when God forgives, it is only because God chooses to carry our sins himself, to bear the weight and cost of them on his own shoulders. And that, of course, is precisely what Jesus did for us on the cross,

> Surely he took up our pain
>> and bore [or carried] our suffering . . .
> and the LORD has laid on him
>> the iniquity of us all. . . .
> For he bore [or carried] the sin of many,
>> and made intercession for the transgressors. (Is 53:4, 6, 12)

So when Paul tells us that the Spirit of God will produce the fruit of patience in our lives, he is reminding us that the God of the Bible is the God who has borne our sin, who carried it himself in the person of his Son, taking upon his own shoulders his righteous anger against all evil and wickedness. That is the true cost of God's patience. And that leads us directly to Jesus.

The Patience of Jesus

The patience of Jesus with his disciples was tested a lot, as they were so often slow to understand what he was saying and doing (but I don't think any of us would have done any better). Nevertheless, Jesus persevered with them. Indeed, John begins his account of Jesus' final meal with his disciples like this: "Jesus knew that the hour had come for him to leave this world and go to the Father. Having loved his own who were in the world, he loved them to the end" (Jn 13:1). And on that same occasion, after he had washed their feet, and they had finished the meal, Jesus prayed to his Father, "While I was with them, I protected them and kept them safe by that name you gave me. None has been lost except the one doomed to destruction so that Scripture would be fulfilled" (Jn 17:12). Jesus had persevered with them patiently through all their faults and failings.

And like the prophets of the Old Testament, Jesus weeps over Jerusalem as he thinks of how patiently God had longed to bring them salvation and protection, but they would not turn back to him.

> "Jerusalem, Jerusalem, you who kill the prophets and stone those sent to you, how often I have longed to gather your children together, as a hen gathers her chicks under her wings, and you were not willing." (Mt 23:37)

> As he approached Jerusalem and saw the city, he wept over it and said, "If you, even you, had only known on this day what would bring you peace—but now it is hidden from your eyes." (Lk 19:41-42)

The supreme patience of Jesus is demonstrated, of course, as he endured the violence, cruelty, and injustice of the cross. And he did that precisely in order to "bear/carry" our sins—without retaliation, but trusting in his Father God. In other words, in his suffering and death, Jesus was bearing not only the immediate hostility of those who demanded and carried out his crucifixion, but also the sin of the world, including yours and mine.

Peter sees the patient suffering of Jesus as a model for our own endurance, in words that echo and quote Isaiah 53.

> If you suffer for doing good and you endure it, this is commendable before God. To this you were called, because Christ suffered for you, leaving you an example, that you should follow in his steps.
>
> > "He committed no sin,
> >   and no deceit was found in his mouth."
>
> When they hurled their insults at him, he did not retaliate; when he suffered, he made no threats. Instead, he entrusted himself to him who judges justly. "He himself bore our sins" in his body on the cross. (1 Pet 2:20-24)

Naturally, therefore, if the Spirit of God is the Spirit of Jesus (as the New Testament sometimes says), then this is one of the ways that he will make us more like Christ, by following his example. The fruit of the Spirit will include the quality of patience that reflects how Christ bore the suffering he endured for our salvation.

So that brings us at last to ourselves. We've seen something of the patience of God in the Old Testament and the patience of Christ in the New Testament. What will it look like when that God-like patience grows like fruit in our own lives?

Patience in Christian Living

Let's go back to those two senses of the word that we mentioned at the start. It means both long-suffering (endurance of persecution) and forbearance (forgiveness of one another), and the word is used in both ways in the New Testament.

Endurance of suffering. The Bible teaches us very clearly that God's people will suffer from the hostility of those who are enemies of God and God's people—enemies that may be human or satanic. And so

Christ's example becomes crucial for us. And when we think about Christ's suffering, what matters is not just the fact that he suffered, but the way he endured that suffering.

> Dear friends, do not be surprised at the fiery ordeal that has come on you to test you, as though something strange were happening to you. But rejoice inasmuch as you participate in the sufferings of Christ, so that you may be overjoyed when his glory is revealed. If you are insulted because of the name of Christ, you are blessed, for the Spirit of glory and of God rests on you. . . . If you suffer as a Christian, do not be ashamed, but praise God that you bear that name. . . . So then, those who suffer according to God's will should commit themselves to their faithful Creator and continue to do good. (1 Pet 4:12-14, 16, 19)

The message from these verses is clear. When Christians suffer, there should be:

- No surprise (we have been warned by Jesus and the apostles again and again to expect it).

- No retaliation (because we follow the example of Christ, who did not fight back, not even in words, when he could have called on an army of angels).

- No quitting (when we commit our cause to God, we do not then sit back and wait; we carry on doing what we are called to, doing good).

Paul was equally clear, and he knew what he was talking about from his own experience:

> You, however, know all about my teaching, my way of life, my purpose, faith, patience, love, endurance, persecutions, sufferings—what kinds of things happened to me in Antioch, Iconium and Lystra, the persecutions I endured. Yet the Lord rescued me from all of them. In fact, everyone who wants to live a godly life in Christ Jesus will be persecuted. (2 Tim 3:10-12)

Millions of our Christian sisters and brothers around the world know all about this. They are suffering hatred, discrimination, imprisonment, expulsion from their homes, and being killed in the most horrendous ways—because of their faith in Jesus. For them, the Bible's teaching about enduring suffering is not a theory or a doctrine, but a terrible reality.

We should be praying regularly for them. But we should also pray for courage for ourselves too. If it comes our turn to suffer in any way because of being Christians in a world that is hostile to our faith or disapproves of our biblical convictions and conscience, then we will need the grace and strength to be like Jesus, in the power of the Spirit, and show patient endurance and not angry retaliation (in word or deed). We need this part of the fruit of the Spirit very much—patient endurance.

In the midst of such suffering and persecution, though, even when we are enduring it with patience, there is a legitimate kind of "impatience" too. It is right that we should cry out to God and pray that he would bring it to an end—as he has promised that he will. Down through the ages, including in the Bible itself, people have longed for the day when God will act and bring an end to injustice, oppression, violence, and evil. Their cry goes up, "How long, Sovereign Lord?" (Rev 6:9-11). We long for the day when God will indeed command, "Be still, and know that I am God," and the day when "he makes wars cease to the ends of the earth" (Ps 46:9-10). But until that day, our calling and challenge is to wait, with hope and with joy, because we know our waiting is not in vain.

> We wait in hope for the Lord;
>   he is our help and our shield.
> In him our hearts rejoice,
>   for we trust in his holy name.
> May your unfailing love be with us, Lord,
>   even as we put our hope in you. (Ps 33:20-22)

Forgiveness of one another. Patience also means forbearance with others. It means putting up with the things other people do (or don't do, when you wish they would). It means that you make the effort to "bear with" other people, even when they irritate and annoy you, or worse. Forbearance is when you choose to forgive people, rather than hold a grudge against them. Forbearance is when you choose to overlook something that was hurtful or unkind, rather than fighting back with harsh words or making sure you get even with the one who did you wrong. Forbearance is when you learn to be patient with others, mainly because you are very well aware of your own short-comings and weaknesses. It means you remember that other people are probably also having to be forbearing with you!

That kind of patience is sadly needed more than ever in Christian churches—and even (maybe especially) among Christian leaders. In the world of instant blogging and commenting (and comments on comments), patience seems to be a very neglected virtue. Some people simply can't wait to put their word in, get their point across, speak their mind—however harmful and hurtful it may be. We have become very impatient—in attitudes, communication, and expectations.

You may be a pastor or church leader of some kind. And you know that the work involved in pastoring God's people calls for limitless, supernatural patience. That's simply because people are what they are— all different. We have different personalities and preferences, different likes and dislikes, different visions and ambitions. And just because we are Christians, it doesn't make those things all blend into nice warm fudge. Some people are very easily upset. Some seem to have been born upset. Jesus had a hard enough time with his twelve disciples. Leading even larger groups of his followers can be a tough challenge.

When I became the principal of a Bible college at the age of forty-five, I did not always find it easy to exercise patience with older members of the staff when we had differences of approach or vision—even though I loved them dearly. I tried hard to obey

Paul's instruction to Timothy, "Do not rebuke an older man harshly, but exhort him as if he were your father" (1 Tim 5:1). And I did so partly because I had great respect for some of those older colleagues who had far more missionary experience and wisdom than I ever had. So, even in disagreement with them, I prayed hard for the gift of patience.

They say you should lead a team like a mountaineer has to lead a group of climbers who are roped together: you must only move at the speed of the slowest climber. But what if one climber has tied his end of the rope to a rock and is refusing to move and says we shouldn't be climbing this mountain at all?

Patience! Forbearance!

And even among the rest of us in the church, not leaders but just the so-called ordinary Christians, how easily we get annoyed and upset with each other. We need so much patience to put up with all the people God has brought together in the church. If only they were all like us! But then we have to remember the patience they need to put up with us in return!

There's a silly little poem that goes:

To dwell in love with saints above—
Oh that will be glory!
But to dwell below with saints we know—
Ah! That's a different story!

It can be very hard to exercise this kind of patience with others. It's hard to be like Christ in this way, to let this fruit of his Spirit ripen in our lives. It is fruit, but at the same time we need to work at it. There is effort and struggle involved. Especially if you've been misunderstood, or misinterpreted, or falsely accused, or if you find out that other people are gossiping about you and spreading rumors. That's when our patience is really tested. But that's also when it counts.

There's not much value in claiming to be a wonderfully patient person if you have nothing to be patient about.

Patience! Forgiveness!

Paul, apostle and leader that he was, knew all about such things, even from the churches he had founded. And yet he urges us to somehow carry the load, to be the blotting paper for other people's spilt ink, to resist the temptation to fight back and become defensive, bitter, and resentful, or to react with angry threats of resignation.

Paul's words to several of his churches provide some basic instructions for both church members and their leaders. Notice the words that I've put in italics.

> Now we ask you, brothers and sisters, to acknowledge those who work hard among you, who care for you in the Lord and who admonish you. Hold them in the highest regard in love because of their work. Live in peace with each other. And we urge you, brothers and sisters, warn those who are idle and disruptive, encourage the disheartened, help the weak, *be patient with everyone.* Make sure that nobody pays back wrong for wrong, but always strive to do what is good for each other and for everyone else. (1 Thess 5:12-15, emphasis mine)

> I urge you . . . be completely humble and gentle; be *patient, bearing with one another in love.* (Eph 4:1-2, emphasis mine)

> *Bear with each other and forgive* one another if any of you has a grievance against someone. Forgive as the Lord forgave you. (Col 3:13, emphasis mine)

We sometimes sing that hymn, "There is a Green Hill Far Away." It has the line, "He died that we might be forgiven." Amen! That's true. But it's also true that he died that we might be forgivers—forgivers of one another. And that kind of willingness to forgive others is itself a fruit of patience, this tough but tender fruit of the Spirit.

Questions

1. In what ways has God been patient with you in your Christian experience?

2. In what ways do other people have to be patient with you?

3. What situations make you most likely to be impatient with others? At such times, how can you show the fruit of the Spirit in your life in patience?

4. What examples can you think of where Christians in your culture have shown (or are now showing) great patience in the face of persecution and suffering?

5. Choose a text on patience (both as perseverance under suffering, and as forbearance toward other Christians) for further Bible study.

Watch a video from Chris about patience
at **ivpress.com/cultivating-patience.**

5

KINDNESS

If patience is a tough fruit of the Spirit, then kindness is a tender one. It is interesting that Paul puts kindness right after patience. Perhaps that's because he saw both of them as essential qualities of *love*—the first fruit of the Spirit. "Love is patient, love is kind," he said (1 Cor 13:4). That's so true, isn't it? When you love people, you find it easier (or at least a bit less difficult!) to be patient with them. And being kind to others is one of the most noticeable characteristics of a genuinely loving person.

What is kindness, then? What sort of behavior do we have in mind when we say that someone has been kind to us or to others? I think the essence of kindness is being thoughtful for others more than for myself in any particular situation. To be kind means to want to help others, to encourage or comfort them, to do something that serves or benefits them. In order to be kind to others, I need to put myself in their shoes and think what I would most want or need them to do for me—and then do it for them. Kindness seems very close to what Jesus meant when he said that we should do for others whatever we wish others would do for us.

Kindness can be as simple as a pleasant word, or a caring smile. But more importantly, being kind means being willing to *do* something, or to take some action, that helps somebody else even if it might be inconvenient to myself. When others are willing to use some of their precious time to help me out of some difficult or confusing situation, they are being kind. Kindness goes beyond duty—it means doing something you don't *have to do*, but just *choose* to do. Kindness goes beyond reward—it means doing something you won't get paid to do. In fact, real kindness usually costs something and doesn't expect any reward. You do what is kind for its own sake and for the sake of the other person. In that sense, kindness is its own reward.

In the Bible, kindness is often linked with generosity. In fact, the word Paul uses often had that sense: kindness could often mean generously providing for another person's benefit. That's biblical kindness.

"Thank you, *you're very kind*," we sometimes say, when another person has done something that we needed. Notice that we don't just say, "That was a very *kind thing* that you did," even though that is true. Kind deeds are done by people who are themselves kind by nature and character. Kindness, in other words, is not just a term to describe *actions*, but a characteristic that describes *people*—people who habitually behave in a way that blesses and benefits others because that is their character.

And that leads us immediately to the character of God as revealed in the Bible. As with the other items in the fruit of the Spirit, we may not quickly associate kindness with the God of the Old Testament, but in fact it is a very strong element of the character of God that is celebrated there.

Kindness and the Character of God

In the Old Testament, God is often praised for his kindness. There is a beautiful word in Hebrew—*hesed*—which is so rich in meaning that it gets translated in many ways. Very often it is translated as "love," with an emphasis on the faithfulness that is an essential part of genuine love. So sometimes *hesed* is translated "faithful love." Sometimes it can mean "loyalty," when one person acts out of a strong sense of commitment to another person because of the relationship between them. When God acts with *hesed* it can mean that he exercises "mercy" toward people who are in a vulnerable or needy situation, so it is quite close to "compassion," which is another word that occurs very often in the Old Testament.

One of the older ways of translating *hesed* (e.g. in the KJV) is "loving-kindness"—a beautiful old English double word that I wish we still used. And often, *hesed* is simply translated as "kindness," since it does have that active sense of doing something for another person, something that shows thoughtful love in action. When God acts in "kindness" (in *hesed),* it means God is being faithful to his covenant promises, paying careful attention to our needs, acting in generous and merciful love, generously providing everything for our blessing and benefit. Didn't I say it is a beautiful word?

We could give dozens of examples of God's *hesed,* but probably the most famous is the last verse of the twenty-third Psalm. "Surely goodness and mercy [*hesed*] shall follow me all the days of my life" (Ps 23:6, KJV; NIV translates the second word as "love").

David was thinking of God as a shepherd who treats his sheep with kindness, protecting and providing for them. A shepherd is *committed* to caring for his sheep, even at his own cost. And so God will keep his commitment to his "flock," his people, because God himself is the essence of goodness and kindness.

The most repetitive use of the word comes in Psalm 136, where every line ends with the phrase, "his *hesed* is forever." The KJV translates it as "his mercy endureth forever," and the NIV as "his love endures forever" (Ps 136:1). The whole psalm celebrates how God, in his works of creation and redemption, has always acted with trustworthy love, even when his redemptive work included acting in judgment on those who opposed him. Psalm 145 says "The LORD is righteous in all his ways and faithful [kind] in all he does [or, toward all he has made]" (Ps 145:17).

The Israelites really celebrated God's kindness. Their history was full of examples of his "kindnesses" that they could recount.

I will tell of the kindnesses of the Lord,
  the deeds for which he is to be praised,
  according to all the Lord has done for us—
yes, the many good things
  he has done for Israel,
  according to his compassion and many kindnesses. (Is 63:7)

So when Paul wanted to tell people in Lystra what the one true living God is like, he focused on God's kindness: "He has shown kindness by giving you rain from heaven and crops in their seasons; he provides you with plenty of food and fills your hearts with joy" (Acts 14:17).

That is very Old Testament language, even though Paul was addressing people who had no clue about the Bible. But the God Paul was telling them about, the God who was so different from all the many gods they worshiped, is the God who shows his character in what he does—even in his generosity in creation toward all human beings.

Paul was very aware that the kindness of God was "available" to all people, but he was also grieved that as fallen sinners we so easily reject it, and fail to understand that God's patient kindness is meant to lead us to repentance and salvation: "Or do you show contempt for the riches of his kindness, forbearance and patience, not realizing that God's kindness is intended to lead you to repentance?" (Rom 2:4).

And of course, as we would expect, the supreme example of the kindness of God (using the same word as this fruit of the Spirit) was God's gift of his own Son, Jesus: "When the kindness and love of God our Savior appeared, he saved us, not because of righteous things we had done, but because of his mercy" (Titus 3:4-5).

Kindness as a Quality of Those Who Worship God

Since that is what God is like, then those who claim to know God and worship him must show the same character. The Old Testament has several outstanding examples of people showing exceptional kindness, reflecting the kindness of God.

Ruth and Boaz. The book of Ruth is a beautiful story of double kindness: Ruth's kindness for Naomi, and Boaz's kindness for both Ruth and Naomi. Actually, it's triple kindness, if you include the Lord God (meaning Yahweh, the God of Israel). For Naomi prays for the Lord's kindness to be shown to her Moabite daughters-in-law (Ruth 1:8), and as the story unfolds God answers that prayer—at least for Ruth (we are just not told what God may have done for Orpah).

First of all, Ruth shows amazing and self-sacrificial kindness to Naomi, her widowed mother-in-law, by refusing to go back to Moab and leave Naomi to return alone to Bethlehem. Her outburst of loyalty, commitment, and conversion to the God of Israel is one of the most remarkable speeches in the Bible:

> But Ruth replied, "Don't urge me to leave you or to turn back from you. Where you go, I will go, and where you stay I will stay. Your people will be my people and your God my God. Where you die I will die, and there I will be buried. May the Lord deal with me, be it ever so severely, if even death separates you and me." (Ruth 1:16-17)

Then, when Boaz meets Ruth as she is gleaning in his field, he commends her for all she has done for Naomi since the death of her husband and father-in-law, and Ruth in turn expresses great relief and gratitude for his kindness (Ruth 2:11-13). And when Ruth tells Naomi that very evening what happened, Naomi bursts out, "'The Lord bless him!' Naomi said to her daughter-in-law. 'He has not stopped showing his kindness *[hesed]* to the living and the dead.' She added, 'That man is our close relative; he is one of our guardian-redeemers'" (Ruth 2:20).

In the next episode, Ruth (on the instruction of Naomi) lies down beside the sleeping Boaz in the middle of the night. And then, when Boaz wakes up very startled (as you would be), and Ruth asks him to marry her, we hear the word *hesed* again. It is quite surprising. You might think Boaz would rebuke Ruth for her embarrassing action and tell her to get up and go home immediately before anybody noticed her there. But no! He *blesses* her: "'The LORD bless you, my daughter,' he replied. 'This kindness *[hesed]* is greater than that which you showed earlier: You have not run after the younger men, whether rich or poor. And now, my daughter, don't be afraid. I will do for you all you ask'" (Ruth 3:10-11).

What "kindness" did Boaz possibly mean? How was Ruth acting in a way that was in any sense "kind" to Boaz? Well, there was the fact (possibly flattering) that she had chosen to ask *him* to marry her (though he was old enough to be her father), when she could have had any young man of her own age. But more than that, he realized that in asking him to marry her as a "guardian-redeemer," she was actually doing "kindness" to Naomi and her deceased husband, Elimelech. For if she could have a son with Boaz, then that son would carry the family name and property of Elimelech. And that explains also why Boaz's willingness to take her as his wife was also seen as a very righteous and kind action for which he is praised (Ruth 4:11-12). So Ruth's action in asking Boaz to marry her was an act of kindness to the family of Elimelech and Naomi, and Boaz's action in agreeing to do so (after some delay) was his act of kindness to them also.

So all in all, the book of Ruth is a story of *hesed*—kindness in action from beginning to end. Boaz and Ruth model the kindness of God. That is how God behaves, and that is how his servants should behave, whether native-born Israelites like Boaz, or converted foreigners like Ruth. Both of them went beyond what was normal or expected in their own cultures. Both of them took considerable risks. And they did so in order to show kindness to someone in dire need. Exactly like God.

David. The friendship between David and Jonathan, son of King Saul, is legendary. They both knew that Saul was determined to kill David if he could. But they also knew that David had been anointed to be king in Saul's place eventually. That would have been a big threat to Jonathan who, as Saul's son, could have expected (and wanted) to be the next king. So Jonathan asks David to swear lifelong loyalty to him and his family—no matter what would happen. His words explicitly ask David to model himself on God in doing so:

> "Show me unfailing kindness *[hesed]* like the LORD's kindness as long as I live, so that I may not be killed, and do not ever cut off your kindness from my family—not even when the LORD has cut off every one of David's enemies from the face of the earth."
>
> So Jonathan made a covenant with the house of David, saying, "May the LORD call David's enemies to account." And Jonathan had David reaffirm his oath out of love for him, because he loved him as he loved himself. (1 Sam 20:14-17)

Later, when Saul and Jonathan had both died in battle with the Philistines and David had become king of all the tribes of Israel, David remembered that promise to Jonathan, and the very terms in which it had been made:

> David asked, "Is there anyone still left of the house of Saul to whom I can show kindness *[hesed]* for Jonathan's sake?"
>
> Now there was a servant of Saul's household named Ziba. They summoned him to appear before David, and the king said to him, "Are you Ziba?"
>
> "At your service," he replied.
>
> The king asked, "Is there no one still alive from the house of Saul to whom I can show God's kindness?"
>
> Ziba answered the king, "There is still a son of Jonathan; he is lame in both feet."

"Where is he?" the king asked.

Ziba answered, "He is at the house of Makir son of Ammiel in Lo Debar."

So King David had him brought from Lo Debar, from the house of Makir son of Ammiel.

When Mephibosheth son of Jonathan, the son of Saul, came to David, he bowed down to pay him honor.

David said, "Mephibosheth!"

"At your service," he replied.

"Don't be afraid," David said to him, "for I will surely show you kindness for the sake of your father Jonathan. I will restore to you all the land that belonged to your grandfather Saul, and you will always eat at my table." (2 Sam 9:1-7)

So the Old Testament, then, taught that *hesed*—kindness—was part of the character of the God of Israel, and should also therefore be part of the character of his people. Faithful love and kindness is what God wants to see being exercised on earth, for that is what he delights in, as several prophets spell out very clearly:

This is what the Lord says:

"Let not the wise boast of their wisdom
    or the strong boast of their strength
    or the rich boast of their riches,
but let the one who boasts boast about this:
    that they have the understanding to know me,
that I am the Lord, who exercises kindness *[hesed]*,
    justice and righteousness on earth,
    for in these I delight,"
        declares the Lord. (Jer 9:23-24)

He has told you, O mortal, what is good;
    and what does the Lord require of you

but to do justice, and to love kindness *[hesed]*,
   and to walk humbly with your God? (Mic 6:8; NRSV)

"This is what the LORD Almighty said: 'Administer true justice;
   show mercy *[hesed]* and compassion to one another.'" (Zech 7:9)

The Wisdom literature goes beyond seeing this simply as a command. It points out that when we do actions that are kind, we not only imitate God, we are actually doing such things *to* God. The word *hesed* does not occur in all of the following texts (sometimes it is the word for compassion which is very close), but the sense of generous kindness to others, especially the needy, is clear.

Those who are kind benefit themselves,
   but the cruel bring ruin on themselves. (Prov 11:17)

It is a sin to despise one's neighbor,
   but blessed is the one who is kind to the needy. (Prov 14:21)

Whoever oppresses the poor shows contempt for their Maker,
   but whoever is kind to the needy honors God. (Prov 14:31)

Whoever is kind to the poor lends to the LORD,
   and he will reward them for what they have done. (Prov 19:17)

Kindness and the Example of Jesus

If kindness is essentially loving others enough to put their needs before your own, then Jesus was kindness incarnate—kindness on two legs.

I have a friend who says he wants to write a book on the life of Jesus and call it "a theology of interruptions." Because, he says, so many of the things that Jesus said or did in the Gospel stories happened because somebody interrupted him when he was actually doing something else, or on a journey, or visiting, or eating. Yet Jesus responded to these interruptions not with irritation and dismissal but with kindness and warmth. And in many cases he showed this respectful kindness to people whom society typically rejected and shunned.

Think of the woman with bleeding, interrupting him on the way to an urgent medical emergency; think of the parents bringing their children when his disciples were wanting to get on with their private lessons; think of blind Bartimaeus who kept shouting over the crowd until Jesus stopped; think of the Syro-Phoenician woman who wouldn't take no for an answer; think of the woman who anointed his feet at a meal, and scandalized the host. Even in Jesus' excruciating agony on the cross, he was thinking of the needs of his mother. And after his resurrection, he knew that hungry fishermen needed a good breakfast after a night at sea.

And all these examples of the kindness of Jesus were not just because he was "a very nice man," or just the kind of person who always seems to be gently smiling in the background. Jesus could use some very strong words and actions against religious leaders and hypocrites. But to the poor, the sick, and the marginalized—people that everybody else pushed aside—to such people Jesus showed extraordinary kindness and gave precious time and attention to their needs. In fact, Jesus crossed barriers and broke down social taboos to show such kindness, by eating and drinking with people whom polite society despised.

So if being a disciple of Jesus means that I ought to follow his example, why do I so often *fail* to take the time to be kind to others in daily life? Even though I'd like to think that I'm generally a kindly sort of fellow, I know that there are many—far too many—occasions when I *could* show some kindness to another person, but don't. Probably nobody notices, but I feel guilty about it inside. Why does it happen? Well I can answer my own question, and maybe you would answer differently, but it is certainly a challenging question to ask.

Often it's because I'm too busy and don't want to be interrupted. I've got things to do, people to see, work to get done. I'm out and about, I'm going somewhere, and I have an agenda and a schedule and time is precious. So the moment flies past when I could stop and just talk for a while to that homeless person, or when I could go over and offer to help that stranger looking a bit lost. I didn't do anybody any harm, but there was a kindness I *could* have done, and it got left undone. I was not willing to let my life be interrupted in order to show kindness to someone else. Not very like Jesus.

Sometimes it's because I'm being self-protective. When I travel, it seems almost necessary to go into "flight mode" and just push ahead: *Don't cross me, I've gotta do what I've gotta do.* There is so much inconvenience and hassle involved in traveling these days that it easily makes me self-absorbed, just concentrating on my own immediate needs and urgency. At such times, I need to remind myself (since Christ lives in me) how I should be behaving toward others around me—even strangers, and even when I'm tired and under pressure (as Jesus must have been). The challenge of exercising kindness, even in stressful circumstances, has to be faced. And it's a challenge that I know I too frequently fail.

Kindness as a Habit of Life

We need to remember that kindness is part of the fruit of the Spirit precisely because it *doesn't* come naturally (even though it's true that some people seem to be just more naturally kind than others). But the sort of kindness Paul is talking about is not "natural," but "spiritual," in the sense that it comes from being filled with God's Spirit.

Such kindness is *fruit* (it grows because of the life of the Spirit within us), but it also has to be *cultivated*. It has to become a *habit* that builds into our *character*.

How do you know something has become a habit? Only when it becomes more natural to say and do what is kind than not to. It has become a habit when you don't have to stop and think and check the many negative reasons before offering to help someone else. It has become a habit if we feel really miserable and self-accusing when, for whatever reason, we *fail* to do and say what is kind, or (even worse) when we behave in ways that we know were downright unkind. At such moments we should be challenging ourselves, *How could I possibly do that? How could I, as a Christian, be so unkind?* And then, of course, we should come back to the Lord to ask for forgiveness and grace. For we all fail at times. But if kindness as the fruit of the Spirit is beginning to grow within us, then we will notice the failure far more painfully and want to ask for grace to do better next time.

So as we go out into each day, with its travel and its work, and its constant rubbing of shoulders with other people, why don't we ask God for opportunities to show kindness?

- Who can I thank today—at home, or in shops, or at work, or while traveling?

- Where can I give a smile or a word of appreciation, for example, to those who clean the streets?

- What will I do if I meet someone in need? Am I prepared in advance to try to help if I can? Have I got some money, or a snack, ready to give?

- Who can I show "the kindness of the Lord" to?

Here is something that may help us move in that direction. Actually, it is one of the most challenging combinations of verses that I have come across in terms of personal behavior. I first heard John Stott preaching on these verses, and his words have stuck with me ever since.

There are two places in Colossians 3 where Paul begins a sentence with, "Whatever you do," which simply means, "in *everything* you do"! The first is: "Whatever you do, whether in word or deed, *do it all in the name of the Lord Jesus*" (Col 3:17, emphasis mine). Now, to do something "in the name of" Jesus means that I am doing something that he would do if he were present. It means that I am acting as though Christ himself were acting in and through me. So the question that this startling text raises in our minds is this: *If I were Christ*, what would I do for that other person? What would Jesus do in this situation? And what, therefore, ought I to do, since I should be acting "in the name of the Lord Jesus"?

The second example from Colossians 3 is: "Whatever you do ... [do it] *as working for the Lord*" (Col 3:23, emphasis mine). That means that I should act *as if the other person were Christ*. What I am doing to or for the other person, I am doing to or for him. Paul was writing this to Christian slaves working for Christian and non-Christian masters. But Paul tells them very clearly that even slaves could *serve Christ* by working hard and honestly for their masters. So this raises another startling and balancing question in our minds: If that person were Christ, what would I do for him or her? How would I behave right now if that were Christ there in front of me? Supposing then we lived each day with those two questions in our minds:

- What would I do for people if *I* were Christ?
- What would I do for people if *they* were Christ?

Wouldn't that make a difference in how we treat other people? What lengths of kindness would we show to others if we asked ourselves those questions and lived out the answers? Even as I write this and remember that teaching of Paul, through the preaching of John Stott, I feel personally convicted yet again. None of us lives up to that standard, do we? But should it not be the goal we aim for?

Richard Wurmband, the Romanian pastor who was imprisoned and tortured under the Communist regime, tells of how one day he was back in a cell with other people after he had been tortured. It was freezing cold and he was hugging his only blanket for warmth. Then he saw another prisoner shivering with cold in the corner with no blanket. He hugged his own blanket more closely to himself, until the thought came into his mind, *If that were Christ, would you give him your blanket?* The question answered itself. He gave the man his blanket (and later, after he was freed, he wrote a book with that question as the title).

That quality of self-denying kindness is not only what it means to be Christlike, it is also deeply attractive to others because it bears witness to the One who lives within us and whose Spirit is bearing fruit in our lives.

Anita Roddick, author of *A Revolution in Kindness*, says, "The end result of kindness is that it draws people to you."

Well, that may be true. But I think we can say, with far greater conviction and for a far better reason, "The end result of kindness is that it draws people to Christ."

Questions

1. List the number of ways you have experienced the kindness of the Lord in your life. What effect does that have on how ready you are to show kindness to others?

2. In your culture, what does kindness look like in practice? Is there any difference between kindness as fruit of the Spirit, and just ordinary "being nice"?

3. What passages of the Bible encourage people to show kindness to one another?

Watch a video from Chris about kindness
at **ivpress.com/cultivating-kindness**.

6

GOODNESS

Paul puts kindness and goodness together, and of course they
have a lot in common. One thing that the Bible often associates with
both goodness and kindness is generosity. Jesus told a story about a
vineyard owner who employed men to work in his vineyard. Some
worked all day and got their one-day's wages. Others had been employed only for the last hour or two of the day, but the owner gave
them a whole day's wages too. The earlier workers complained it
wasn't fair, but the owner said to them, "Are you envious because I am
generous?" (Mt 20:15, emphasis mine). And the word Jesus used there
is the same as the one Paul uses—"*good.*" Jesus is saying that good
people don't always worry about what is strictly *fair*, but rather like
to err on the side of generosity and kindness. It was not the men's
fault that they had been hired only toward the end of the day. And
they needed a day's wage to be able to buy food for their families. So
the owner chooses to be *good* (generous) toward their needs, rather
than strictly *fair* in relation to all the workers and pay them only a
fraction of what the others got.

So when we associate the word "good" with a title or function (for
example a good parent, or a good teacher, or a good police officer, or a
good doctor), we sometime mean not only that the person is "good at"

something (competent), but also that the person knows how to go beyond the strict limits of what the role demands and acts with some grace and generosity of spirit as well, "out of the goodness of the heart," as we sometimes say.

But what lies at the heart of "goodness"? What quality do we see in someone when we say—"He is a really good man," or "she is a really good woman"? I think one key thing would be integrity—an absence of any kind of guile or deception. Truly good people are WYSIWYG (What You See Is What You Get). They are in reality all they appear to be. Their words and behavior on the outside matches what is going on inside. There is no sham or pretense. When they do good, it is not just some kind of playacting to get a good name, or a good photo-op, or a good sound bite. Good people do what they do simply because it is the *right thing* to do. Goodness is close to what it means to be "pure in heart." Goodness has a transparent quality. Most simply, you can depend on good people to be and do what they say (they keep their word)—and to do what is right (simply because it is the right thing to do).

As before, since this is part of the fruit of the Spirit of God, we can begin by looking at the source of all goodness, God himself.

God Is Good

African Christians have a response they like to use together, sometimes formally in worship, and sometimes just when they meet and greet one another casually.

"God is good,"
"All the time!"
"All the time,"
"God is good!"

That is a fundamental and frequent affirmation in the Bible too. It's all over the Psalms—"Give thanks to the LORD, for he is good" (Ps 136:1) and "You are good, and what you do is good" (Ps 119:68). When Moses asked God to show him his glory, God replied by saying, "I will cause all my goodness to pass in front of you, and I will proclaim my name, the LORD" (Ex 33:19). What an experience that must have been for Moses, and no wonder his face was radiant after that! (Ex 34:5-7; 29-35). So it's no wonder that when he composed one of his songs, Moses multiplied words to describe God's goodness.

> He is the Rock, his works are perfect,
>   and all his ways are just.
> A faithful God who does no wrong,
>   upright and just is he. (Deut 32:4)

So then, to say that God is good means what we have just been saying above. God is generous and trustworthy, without any deception or crookedness, and he is like that always, through and through like a solid rock, in his own character and in all his actions. The goodness of God is axiomatic in the Bible. That means, like an axiom in mathematics, it is an affirmed truth that is foundational to all the other deductions and calculations you may make. No matter what the circumstances are or appear to be, God *is* good and God *does* good.

Even when bad things happen, God can overrule that evil to bring about good results—as Joseph told his brothers. "You intended to harm me *[Heb. You intended it for evil]*, but God intended it for good to accomplish what is now being done, the saving of many lives" (Gen 50:20).

Now, be careful. That does not mean that the bad things people do are somehow not evil anymore. It does not mean that God makes evil good in itself. That would be a complete contradiction. It does not mean that there is essentially no difference between good and evil for "it will all turn out all right in the end." That kind of thinking dissolves the fundamental biblical distinction between good and evil. No. Joseph did not try to excuse or minimize or deny the evil that his brothers had done. Selling him into slavery was a desperately wicked act to do to a brother. Evil is evil. And they meant it to be evil when they did it. But what Joseph's words do mean is that God's goodness is sovereign (because the good God reigns), and God has the power to bring good results out of the evil that people intend and perpetrate. God's goodness overcomes evil for good. God is in charge and God is good.

Models of Goodness

If God is utterly good, then it's not surprising that people who live close to God reflect his character and are marked by this same quality. Daniel is a good example of goodness in action.

Daniel was a political administrator, working for the government of Babylon, and then for the government of Persia at the end of his life. And in his daily life and work at the office, he had "a spirit of excellence" (that's the phrase in Hebrew, translated "exceptional qualities" in the NIV). His enemies "could find no corruption in him, because he was trustworthy and neither corrupt nor negligent" (Dan 6:3-4).

That is a remarkable description. Daniel was a man who could be trusted at work (and it was not "Christian work," but ordinary secular work in the service of the government). His boss could trust him, and those working under him could trust him. His goodness and integrity were transparent and evident to all.

But people who are good and upright in the workplace like that can be unpopular with those who are corrupt and want to use their work as a means of getting rich or powerful. And it seems Daniel was an obstacle to the ambitions of other people in the government service, so they hated him and plotted against him. In Daniel 6, they came up with a plan to entrap him. They knew they could not find a weakness in his moral behavior at work, so they decided to make use of his strength in his personal life of worship and prayer. They got the king to pass a decree that nobody should pray to any god except him for a month (a crazy idea, but the king, in his vanity, fell for it).

So when that decree was passed, Daniel was faced with the decision: either to carry on with his daily habit of prayer to the God of Israel, or to give it up for a month and pray to the king—who was not so much a false god as no god at all! He chose to do what was right in the sight of God and continued his daily prayers, in spite of the threat that it could cost him his career and possibly his life. In Daniel chapter 6, Daniel was already an old man, but this habit of doing what was right, even if it was risky, was something he and his friends had cultivated since their earliest youth in chapter 1. On this occasion, it got him thrown into the den of lions, where the God to whom he prayed saved his life (much to the relief of the king).

That seems to be another strong element of biblical goodness—being committed to doing the right thing *even when it costs or hurts.* "Good" people are those who resist the temptation to take the easy way out of a tough situation. Even when it is difficult or dangerous to do the right thing, they do it anyway. They persevere in doing what they know to be right, no matter what the consequences. For that reason good people are usually also courageous, and sometimes they do indeed pay a heavy price for their integrity.

Another word that is very close to goodness in the Old Testament is righteousness. The righteous person is the one who responds to the love, grace, and salvation of God by seeking to live in God's way and do what is right in God's eyes—*not* in an effort to earn God's favor, but out of grateful response to God's blessing. There are several descriptions in the Old Testament of the typical righteous person. One of the clearest is in Psalm 15:

> LORD, who may dwell in your sacred tent?
>   Who may live on your holy mountain?
>
> The one whose walk is blameless,
>   who does what is righteous,
>   who speaks the truth from their heart;

whose tongue utters no slander,
   who does no wrong to a neighbor,
   and casts no slur on others;
who despises a vile person
   but honors those who fear the Lord;
who keeps an oath even when it hurts,
   and does not change their mind;
who lends money to the poor without interest;
   who does not accept a bribe against the innocent.

Whoever does these things
   will never be shaken. (Ps 15:1-15)

Notice that line about keeping your promise even when it hurts. That is a mark of biblical goodness. The good man or woman resists the temptation to find some way out of keeping a promise, or speaking the truth, or doing the honest thing. Nearly always, there is some alternative option available. But the good choice is the right choice, even when it's the hard one.

Jesus "Went Around Doing Good"

That is how Peter described Jesus to Cornelius and his family (Acts 10:38). It doesn't mean *only* that Jesus did a lot of kind and caring things for people (of course he did). It also means that Jesus did what was right. Jesus did what he knew God his Father wanted him to do, even when he could have chosen an easy way out. Jesus was a man of goodness, seen in his righteous integrity. He refused to deviate from what he knew was the Father's will for him.

Think of the number of times Jesus was offered an alternative—an easy way out—or when he faced the choice of taking a different route than the way of the cross.

- The devil tempted him three times to take an easier route—through popularity, or spectacular death-defying stunts, or political power.

But Jesus resisted and chose the path of the suffering servant and the obedient Son—the identity that his Father had affirmed at his baptism.

- Simon Peter tried to deflect him away from the whole idea of suffering and crucifixion. But Jesus rebuked him.

- His beloved mother and brothers tried to get him to come home and give up his embarrassing and risky public ministry. But Jesus claimed that his true mother and brothers and sisters were those who did the will of his Father.

- In the Garden of Gethsemane, he longed desperately for any other option than what lay ahead of him the next day. But he chose to do the Father's will.

- When they arrested him, he knew he could have called on a legion of angels to rescue him, but he did not.

- Even Pontius Pilate dangled the possibility of release before Jesus, when he was staring the cross in the face. But Jesus refused.

So, through all these temptations and diversions, Jesus demonstrated his "goodness" through his integrity and determination to do what was right, to do the will of his Father. He was, as Paul said, "obedient to death" (Phil 2:8).

Doing Good, as the Fruit of the Spirit within Us

So the goodness of God is seen in the goodness of Jesus, and that is why this too is fruit of the Spirit. Goodness comes from the life of God within us. What Jesus did came from who Jesus was in his own heart and mind and motives. Goodness is a heart thing. It comes from inside. What we are on the outside is like "fruit," and fruit is the evidence of what is going on inside—the nature of the tree itself.

Here's how Jesus makes this point very clearly:

No good tree bears bad fruit, nor does a bad tree bear good fruit. Each tree is recognized by its own fruit. . . . A good man brings good things out of the good stored up in his heart, and an evil man brings evil things out of the evil stored up in his heart. For the mouth speaks what the heart is full of. (Lk 6:43-45)

What we do shows what we are. Our actions (on the outside) show what (or rather who) is on the inside. So if Christ, through his Holy Spirit, takes up residence in our lives, then more and more we begin to show the character of Jesus in the way we think, speak, and act. Not that we are ever perfect (in this life), but the fruit begins to grow.

So it is out of the deep well of goodness in the heart, flowing from the life of the Spirit of God living within us and modeled by Jesus himself, that we draw the water that will irrigate the fruit of the Spirit, by *being* good in our thoughts, attitudes, words, and actions, and by *doing* good—not as "do-gooders" (inferring busybodies), but as "good-doers."

And not only does the goodness of the Holy Spirit grow within ourselves, we also begin to notice and encourage that same fruit in others. We know that it is only by the grace of God that we are being changed. And therefore when we see the grace of God at work in other people's lives, we are filled with joy. We see the family likeness, because we are children of the same Father, disciples of the same Lord, and indwelt by the same Spirit.

This ability to see goodness at work in other people is what marked out Barnabas. It's easy to like Barnabas because he was, as his name meant, a great encourager of others, including Saul of Tarsus before he became known as the Apostle Paul.

On one occasion Barnabas was sent on a special mission from Jerusalem to Antioch to inspect what was happening there. People who were not Jews (the Gentiles) were coming to faith in Jesus as the gospel was preached to them as well. The church in Antioch must have seemed strange and unfamiliar to Jewish people, since the Gentile believers would not be following Jewish customs, and their way of worshiping must have been very different too. So they sent Barnabas to check it out. And Luke tells us, "When he arrived and saw what the grace of God had done, he was glad . . ." (Acts 11:23).

I love that! Barnabas's first instinct was not to question or criticize or tell these new Gentile Christians what they were doing wrong. No, when he saw clear evidence that the grace of God was at work in these other people—no matter how different they were from himself—he was glad! And that must be why Luke immediately gives us a character sketch of Barnabas in these words: "He was a *good man*, full of the Holy Spirit and faith," and because of that unselfish quality of goodness in Barnabas, the work of the church went on, people were encouraged, and "a great number of people were brought to the Lord" (Acts 11:24, emphasis mine).

We could use many more people like Barnabas in the church, people who simply and humbly show that kind of goodness—goodness born of the Holy Spirit that enables them to recognize the grace of God even in unfamiliar places and people.

Doing Good as an Essential Part of Christian Living

In the Sermon on the Mount, Jesus teaches his disciples. Now "disciples" means those who have responded to his invitation to repent and believe the good news about the reign of God, and who then commit themselves to live according to the standards and values of the kingdom of God. Living within the kingdom of God means living under God's reign—living with God as king. And that means a radical change of life and attitudes, in order to reflect or imitate God our heavenly Father. The Sermon on the Mount is not a whole *new set of rules*. It is rather a description of a *new quality of life*. It describes the thinking and behavior that should characterize the followers of Jesus when they submit to God's reign in their lives and acknowledge that Jesus himself is Lord and King over all.

That kind of life will be like salt, says Jesus. Salt was used to stop meat or fish from going rotten. Salt counteracted the natural process of decay and corruption. So Jesus implies that in a world that is rotten and corrupt through sin, his disciples should be people who stand against that by the way they live and speak. We are to be different, as distinctive as salt is from rottenness.

And then he told his disciples, "You are the light of the world" (Mt 5:14). They must have been rather shocked at such a statement! What did Jesus mean? Did he mean that they would be preachers of the truth of the gospel that would bring light to people in the darkness of ignorance and sin? Yes, of course he would have included that in the overall task of the apostolic mission—as Paul explains using the same metaphor in 2 Corinthians 4:4-6. But look at what Jesus actually stresses when he explains what he means by "light." He did not say, "let your light shine so that people will hear your personal testimony, or listen to your great preaching." No, this is what he said: "Let your light shine before others, that they may see *your good deeds* and glorify your Father in heaven" (Mt 5:16, emphasis mine).

When Jesus talks here about "light" he is speaking about *lives* (not just words). He is calling for lives that are attractive by being filled with goodness, mercy, love, compassion, and justice. The word translated "good" is *kalos*, which also means "beautiful," not just morally upright. That kind of *practical goodness* will draw people to Christ and ultimately to know and glorify God the Father.

As he so often did, when Jesus told his disciples that they were the "light of the world," he was drawing on a strong Old Testament tradition. God had called Israel to be a "light to the nations" (Is 51:4). And that role included the quality of their lives as a society. "Light" had a strongly ethical and social meaning. Listen to Isaiah and notice the combination of "light" and "righteousness" in the sense explained above. Light shines from people committed to compassion and justice.

Is not this the kind of fasting I have chosen:
to loose the chains of injustice
    and untie the cords of the yoke,
to set the oppressed free
    and break every yoke?
Is it not to share your food with the hungry
    and to provide the poor wanderer with shelter—
when you see the naked, to clothe them,
    and not to turn away from your own flesh and blood?
Then *your light* will break forth like the dawn,
    and your healing will quickly appear;
then *your righteousness* will go before you, . . .
if you spend yourselves in behalf of the hungry
    and satisfy the needs of the oppressed,
then *your light* will rise in the darkness,
    and your night will become like the noonday. (Is 58:6-8, 10,
      emphasis mine)

A little later Isaiah adds that such light—that is, the light of compassion, justice, and practical care for the needy—not only reflects the light of God's own presence and glory among his people, but it will also draw the nations. That is a vision that reflects God's promise to Abraham that the nations would be blessed. This is "light" that is missionally attractive (Is 60:1-3). When God's people live in God's way, and model the goodness of God for others, then that will bring others to see the truth about God and to know and glorify him for themselves. Doesn't that tie in exactly with what Jesus said about shining as the light of the world by doing good deeds?

So then in the Old Testament, God commanded Israel to be a people committed to practical, down-to-earth exercise of compassion and justice. And Jesus both endorsed that mandate for his disciples and indeed radically deepened it. And then in the Great Commission,

Jesus commanded them to pass that teaching on to the new disciples they would make ("teaching them to obey everything I have commanded you" [Mt 28:20]). Both in their life as a community of disciples, and in their mission of making disciples, they must reflect the goodness of the God who cares for the poor and needy, the goodness of the God who defends the cause of the widow and orphan. That must be the quality of our goodness also, as disciples of Jesus, with the life of Christ living in us by his Spirit.

The apostle Paul also had a great deal to say about the importance of Christians being people who do good. We sometimes don't emphasize this as much as we should. In fact, sometimes we seem to be afraid to take seriously (or preach about) what Paul says about good works in the life of Christians (which is a lot, as we shall see in a moment). The reason for that, of course, is that we are very committed to the doctrine of "justification by grace alone through faith alone." We affirm strongly that *we cannot be saved* by good works. And so we then soft-pedal all that Jesus, Paul, and the rest of the New Testament actually say about doing good. We don't want to give the impression that our own good works can earn us salvation, which is, of course, true and is a vitally important part of the gospel of grace. But Paul, who was so insistent that we cannot be saved *by* good works, was equally insistent that we are saved *in order to do* good works. We are not, and could never be, saved *by* any amount of good works. But we are saved by God's grace *in order to* live transformed lives in which doing good is a key part.

Paul puts the two truths side by side in Ephesians 2, in the phrases I've marked in italics:

> For it is by grace you have been saved, through faith—and this is not from yourselves, it is the gift of God—*not by works*, so that no one can boast. For we are God's handiwork, created in Christ Jesus *to do good works*, which God prepared in advance for us to do. (Eph 2:8-10, emphasis mine)

He does the same in his letter to Titus—making both the negative and the positive point very clearly (as shown in the phrases I have marked in italics):

> But when the kindness and love of God our Savior appeared, *he saved us, not because of righteous things we had done, but because of his mercy.* He saved us through the washing of rebirth and renewal by the Holy Spirit, whom he poured out on us generously through Jesus Christ our Savior, so that, having been justified by his grace, we might become heirs having the hope of eternal life. This is a trustworthy saying. And I want you to stress these things, *so that those who have trusted in God may be careful to devote themselves to doing what is good.* (Titus 3:4-8, emphasis mine)

So long as we are crystal clear that good works are not the source or grounds for our salvation, Paul insists that once we have experienced God's salvation we are called to respond to his saving grace and redeeming love by living lives that are characterized by goodness. As people saved by grace, we are to be people committed to being and doing what is good and right, in our personal and public lives, in the church and in the world.

I said above that Paul had a lot to say about "doing good." He makes that point in most of his letters with a remarkable concentration of examples in the small letter to Titus.

> Hate what is evil; *cling to what is good.* (Rom 12:9, emphasis mine)

> God is able to bless you abundantly, so that in all things at all times, having all that you need, you will abound in *every good work* [i.e. in the good work of generosity]. (2 Cor 9:8, emphasis mine)

> Let us not become weary in *doing good* . . . as we have opportunity, let us do good to all people, especially to those who belong to the family of believers. (Gal 6:9-10, emphasis mine)

Live a life worthy of the Lord and please him in every way: bearing fruit in *every good work.* (Col 1:10, emphasis mine)

As for you, brothers and sisters, never tire of *doing what is good.* (2 Thess 3:13, emphasis mine)

[An elder] must be hospitable, one who *loves what is good,* who is self-controlled, upright, holy and disciplined. (Titus 1:8, emphasis mine)

Teach the older women to be reverent in the way they live, not to be slanderers or addicted to much wine, but to *teach what is good.* (Titus 2:3, emphasis mine)

In everything set them an example by *doing what is good.* (Titus 2:7, emphasis mine)

Jesus Christ, who gave himself for us to redeem us from all wickedness and to purify for himself a people that are his very own, *eager to do what is good.* (Titus 2:13-14, emphasis mine)

Remind the people to be subject to rulers and authorities, to be obedient, to be *ready to do whatever is good,* to slander no one, to be peaceable and considerate, and always to be gentle towards everyone. (Titus 3:1-2, emphasis mine)

So that those who have trusted in God may be careful *to devote themselves to doing what is good.* (Titus 3:8, emphasis mine)

Our people must learn to *devote themselves to doing what is good.* (Titus 3:14, emphasis mine)

Why does Paul put such strong emphasis on Christians being people who do good works? Why, in other words, is goodness an essential part of the fruit of the Spirit, which should become evident in our lives in our character, attitudes, thinking, and behavior?

One major reason is that this reflects the nature and truth of the gospel. In fact, it reflects the dynamic of the cross and resurrection. When Paul says: "Do not be overcome by evil, *but overcome evil with good*" (Rom 12:21, emphasis mine), he is echoing exactly what God did at the cross. For at the cross, the goodness of God overcame all the human and satanic evil in creation by bearing it in himself in the person of Jesus. The cross is the ultimate expression of the goodness of God, and the resurrection proved its victory. *Goodness overcomes evil.* That is the ultimate whole story of the Bible. That is the heart of the gospel. And that is our hope for the future.

So when we respond to the evil in the world by acting in kindness and goodness, we are not only bearing the supernatural fruit of the Spirit of God within us, we are also living in the power of the cross and resurrection, and we are anticipating the final victory of God's goodness over all the evil in the universe. Indeed, we are *applying* that victory of the cross and resurrection. It is *not* (not at all, not ever) that we are doing good in order to earn our salvation. But rather that in doing good we demonstrate the saving and transforming power of the gospel.

So you see, the cross and resurrection are not just the proof of *God's* goodness, they are also the source and pattern of any and all goodness *we* can do as Christians.

So let us pray for the power of the Spirit to bear this fruit of the Spirit, and cultivate it in our daily lives, especially in the public world of our work and in all our social relationships.

Do what is good! Do what is right! And let God take responsibility for the consequences.

Questions

1. What other characters in the Bible are like Barnabas, "a *good man*, full of the Holy Spirit and faith" (Acts 11:24)? What do they show us about goodness as a fruit of the Spirit?

2. Are there examples of people in your culture—past or present—who have done what is good and right, even when it was hard or costly?

3. How are we to live once we have experienced God's salvation, understanding that good works are not the basis for our salvation?

Watch a video from Chris about goodness
at **ivpress.com/cultivating-goodness**.

7

FAITHFULNESS

"Well done, good and faithful servant . . . " (Mt 25:21, 23).

That is one of the favorite sayings of Jesus that all of his followers long to hear. As we love and serve Christ through our lives, we want to be *faithful* servants. And that is what we can be, says Paul, if we allow the Holy Spirit to bear this portion of his fruit in our lives. But what does it mean? I think there are two connected elements in the word "faithfulness."

On the one hand, being faithful means being *trustworthy and dependable*. A faithful person is a person of honesty and integrity, someone you can rely on. Faithful people keep their word. They do what they promise. They can be trusted not to cheat or deceive.

On the other hand, being faithful means exercising that kind of trustworthy behavior *over a long period of time*. Faithful people have proved that they can be trusted for the long haul. You don't have to check up on them. You don't have to worry that, even if they did a good job last week, they might let you down this week. No, faithful people show that they are routinely dependable in all kinds of ways and all kinds of circumstances. Faithfulness is the character of *somebody you know you can simply rely on all the time*.

And that, surely, is exactly the truth about God. That's why faithfulness is the fruit of God's Spirit at work in us.

The Faithfulness of God

Can you think of anything the Bible says about God more often than this? One of the oldest poems in the Bible describes God as "the Rock," and highlights the qualities that inspired that metaphor:

> Ascribe greatness to our God!
> "The Rock! His work is perfect,
> For all His ways are just;
> *A God of faithfulness* and without injustice,
> Righteous and upright is He." (Deut 32:3-4, NASB,
>   emphasis mine)

The Psalms celebrate it all over the place:

> All the ways of the Lord are loving and faithful
>   toward those who keep the demands of his covenant.
>   (Ps 25:10)

> For the word of the Lord is right and true;
>   he is faithful in all he does.
> The Lord loves righteousness and justice;
>   the earth is full of his unfailing love. (Ps 33:4-5)

> Your love, Lord, reaches to the heavens,
>   your faithfulness to the skies. (Ps 36:5)

Suppose you could have come alongside the Israelites who wrote songs like that, and you were able to ask them, "Excuse me, but *how do you know that*? How can you be so sure that the Lord your God is so faithful?" I think they would have taken you aside, made you sit down, and told you their story—meaning the great story of the people of Israel in the Old Testament.

Look again at those descriptions of God in Psalm 33—faithfulness, justice, love. For an Israelite, the exodus story proved all of them. "You asked about the Lord's faithfulness?" your Israelite friend might say.

"He kept his promise to Abraham when he brought us up out of Egypt. You asked about God's justice? He showed that in bringing judgment on the Egyptians for their economic exploitation and genocidal oppression of our ancestors. You asked about his love? Listen to how God put up with us, in all our grumbling and rebellion in the wilderness; how he gave us food and water and kept us safe from our enemies. That's how I know that God is faithful. Come and sing the psalm with me!"

The Israelites knew their stories and kept on singing about God's faithfulness, simply because God had proved it through the long centuries of their history. They knew God could be trusted, because he'd kept every promise he'd ever made.

So even when the Israelites were suffering under God's judgment for their sin, they still came back and appealed to this characteristic of God and pleaded with him to be faithful to his promises of restoration. God would be faithful. He would keep his promises as well as his threats.

"Great is thy faithfulness." That's the first line of a well-known Christian hymn. But the words actually come right in the middle of the book of Lamentations (Lam 3:23). And that book emerged at the most terrible moment of Israel's Old Testament history, when Jerusalem had been destroyed, the temple burnt, and the people sent in exile under God's judgment because of their sin. Yet even in those horrendous circumstances, even when they were suffering the consequences of *their own* unfaithfulness, they could still affirm the eternal faithfulness of God. So those words come as a shaft of light in the midst of the appalling darkness of the chapters that surround them in the book of Lamentations. God can be trusted, even when hope and faith seem shattered on the rocks of sin and suffering.

The apostle Paul knew those Scriptures, of course, in the depth of his heart and memory. So it is not surprising that he often reminds his readers of God's faithfulness, now proved even more fully in the life, death, and resurrection of Jesus the Messiah.

God is faithful, who has called you into fellowship with his Son, Jesus Christ our Lord. (1 Cor 1:9)

God is faithful; he will not let you be tempted beyond what you can bear. But when you are tempted, he will also provide a way out so that you can endure it. (1 Cor 10:13)

May your whole spirit, soul and body be kept blameless at the coming of our Lord Jesus Christ. The one who calls you is faithful, and he will do it. (1 Thess 5:23-24)

So, God can be trusted. That's for sure.

But can God's people be trusted? Sadly, not much. The story of Old Testament Israel is one of their repeated, grinding, unfaithfulness to God. Israel's unfaithfulness to Yahweh their covenant God is portrayed in the prophets (Hosea and Jeremiah especially) as unfaithfulness in a marriage. And we know that marital unfaithfulness creates pits of betrayal, ingratitude, and pain. That's what God felt when his own faithfulness collided with Israel's unfaithfulness.

Now let's be careful here too. We should not feel self-righteous in condemning the Old Testament Israelites, for the history of the Christian church has not been much better. The unfaithfulness of God's people over the centuries, and the remarkable contrasting faithfulness of God to his people in spite of their failures, is one of the clearest and most constant threads running through both the Bible and church history.

But there were exceptions. There were some men and women in the Old Testament who showed exemplary faithfulness to God and to God's calling on their lives—with long-term, lifelong, costly, dependable obedience, and commitment. Hebrews 11 lists some of the greatest examples of such faith and faithfulness. But let's take just one of them—Moses. I think we can learn a lot from the stories of Moses about what Paul means by faithfulness as the fruit of the Spirit.

The Faithfulness of Moses

The writer to the Hebrews, speaking about Jesus Christ, compares Jesus to Moses in this respect—his faithfulness.

> Therefore, holy brothers and sisters, who share in the heavenly calling, fix your thoughts on Jesus, whom we acknowledge as our apostle and high priest. He was faithful to the one who appointed him, just as *Moses was faithful in all God's house.* (Heb 3:1-2, emphasis mine)

Now that last part of the sentence, referring to Moses, is actually a quote from God himself. Have a look at the story in Numbers 12. Moses was facing a crisis from within his own family. Aaron and Miriam had challenged their brother Moses, but Moses, being a humble man, said nothing. God spoke up in his defense, however, saying:

> "When there is a prophet among you,
>   I, the LORD, reveal myself to them in visions,
>   I speak to them in dreams.
> But this is not true of my servant Moses;
>   *he is faithful in all my house.*
> With him I speak face to face,
>   clearly and not in riddles;
>   he sees the form of the LORD.
> Why then were you not afraid
>   to speak against my servant Moses?" (Num 12:6-8,
>   emphasis mine)

Why did God single out that quality of faithfulness in Moses? Well, if you read the whole narrative in Numbers 11–16, just look at the list of problems Moses had to cope with as a leader:

- Catering problems (Num 11)—how was he supposed to feed them all with meat?

- Confusion over the gifts of the Spirit (Num 11:24-30)—nothing has changed!

- Criticism from his own family about his marriage (Num 12).

- Discouragement from the majority of spies sent to Canaan (Num 13).

- Grumbling rebellion of the whole people (Num 14:1-9).

- Death threats (Num 14:10).

- Mutiny of key tribal leaders (Num 16).

Yet, in the midst of crisis after crisis, Moses stayed faithful to the job God had given him. God reckoned he could trust Moses, even under enormous pressure. That's why it is God himself who commends Moses for his faithfulness.

In these stories in Numbers, I see the faithfulness of Moses in two areas especially, both of which stand as very strong models for the kind of Christian leaders who want to be marked by faithfulness:

A complete lack of selfish jealousy (Num 11). In the course of the story in Numbers 11, two men (Eldad and Medad) did not turn up along with the rest of the elders of Israel when God "shared" the Spirit that he had given to Moses with the wider group so that they could help Moses carry the burden of leadership. They had stayed in the camp (we are not told why; perhaps they were ill, or they forgot what day it was). But God did not leave them out. "Yet the Spirit also rested on them, and they prophesied in the camp" (Num 11:26).

Then somebody ran to tell Moses that two people were prophesying in the camp—without his permission or supervision! This could all get out of control! So Joshua interrupted and said, "Moses, my lord, stop them!" (Num 11:28). Joshua was second in command to Moses. And often people in that position are very anxious to protect the authority of the leader (since their own status depends on keeping the leader in his position). So Joshua thought this unauthorized, unsupervised, charismatic outburst was a threat to Moses (and so, derivatively, to himself perhaps). So his response was classic, "This has got to stop now!"

I love how Moses answered Joshua. I think he must have had a twinkle in his eye as he rebuked him: "Are you jealous for my sake? I wish all the LORD's people were prophets and that the LORD would put his Spirit on them!" (Num 11:29).

If God wanted to spread his gifts around, that was okay for Moses. He didn't need to monopolize the Spirit of God. If others could share in the gifts that God had given to him, so much the better. The more people had a share of the Spirit, the less they would trouble Moses, perhaps, with all their problems. Moses had no urge to bolster his own authority by keeping God's Spirit and gifts to himself. Rather, Moses wanted to serve God and God's people in whatever way God deemed best. He was faithful both to God and to the people. Faithfulness to God and his people means that we aren't jealous of others, or upset when other people exercise spiritual gifts that we like to think are ours. Moses showed his faithfulness in his lack of that kind of selfish jealousy.

A complete lack of selfish ambition (Num 14). Later in the same story, the people rebelled yet again and refused to move forward into the Promised Land. For the second time (the first was at Mount Sinai in Exodus 32–34), God threatened to destroy those people and start again with Moses. In other words, God would still create a people for his purpose, but it would no longer be the children of Israel, descended from Abraham. They would be the "children of Moses."

But Moses refused. When you think of all the hassle and grief he was suffering from these people, it must have been quite a temptation to imagine being rid of them and starting from fresh with just his own family. But no. Moses rejected God's suggestion and instead he pleaded with God to forgive the people. You can read the amazing story in Numbers 14:10-19, and it is told again in Deuteronomy 9:13-29.

So what we see is that Moses had no ambition to build an empire for himself. He had no desire to have the glory of being the founder of a great nation. Rather, his whole life, work, prayer, and passion was to serve the people—*this people*, the people whom God had entrusted to his reluctant leadership since the burning bush. He would not allow even God to deflect him from that calling. That is real faithfulness. For Moses it meant forty years of faithful obedience to God and faithful leadership of a very ungrateful people over two generations, doing a job that he hadn't even wanted in the first place!

I have chosen Moses as a prime example of faithfulness. You could take other biblical characters and make a list of the events in their lives that show this quality of faithfulness. Think of Joseph, Samuel, Ruth, Daniel, Jeremiah. In what ways did they prove their faithfulness in action, as God was at work in their lives?

Faithfulness in the Teaching and Example of Jesus and Paul

Jesus. As Hebrews pointed out, Jesus was faithful as God's Son even more so than Moses was faithful as God's servant. Jesus was faithful to the task he came to accomplish. He did his Father's will and finished the work he was given to do—in spite of all the obstacles and temptations, human and satanic. So, at the end of his life, as he prepared to be obedient even unto death, he could say to his Father, "I have brought you glory on earth by finishing the work you gave me to do" (Jn 17:4).

And so Jesus called for faithfulness among his followers. Following Jesus requires commitment and perseverance. It means denying yourself and taking up the cross. It is not for those who start out with enthusiasm but then quickly turn back. It is not for those who are entangled with all kinds of other priorities. It is not for those who say "Lord! Lord!" to Jesus but never do what he says. It is not for those who want an easy road. The Beatitudes point to a very different quality of life within the kingdom of God that is the opposite of a life of carefree luxury and ease.

That quotation at the start of this chapter ("Well done, good and faithful servant") comes from Jesus' famous parable about the bags of gold entrusted by a master to his servants. The master in the story says those words to the two servants who used what had been entrusted to them in order to bring benefit to their master. They worked with what they had and produced good results for him. And for that reason the master calls them "good and faithful" servants (Mt 25:14-23). They were *good* because they knew the right thing to do and did it, and they were *faithful* because they were trustworthy and did not try to enrich themselves at their employer's expense.

Now that parable, like the others in Matthew 25, is not directly about money as such, but is one of several illustrations that Jesus used to speak about the urgency of the kingdom of God and the responsibilities of those who know and serve the King. But sometimes Jesus did actually speak about money and wealth in literal terms. He had some severe warnings about being addicted to it. But he also insisted that whenever we do handle money in any way, we need to be fully trustworthy, to be people of integrity and honesty. Faithfulness includes being accountable—materially as well as spiritually.

> Whoever can be trusted with very little can also be trusted with much, and whoever is dishonest with very little will also be dishonest with much. So if you have not been trustworthy in handling worldly wealth, who will trust you with true riches? And if you have not been trustworthy with someone else's property, who will give you property of your own?
>
> No one can serve two masters. Either you will hate the one and love the other, or you will be devoted to the one and despise the other. You cannot serve both God and money. (Lk 16:10-13)

Jesus was very clear. The great enemy of serving God is *Mammon*—not just money in itself, but money as a powerful and seductive source of temptation and idolatry. Unfaithfulness over money has been the downfall of so many Christians, and especially Christian leaders.

Faithfulness, then, requires integrity and accountability because it requires *trust*. And you can only really trust someone when they have proved themselves *trustworthy* by being honest, transparent, and accountable in all their dealings. For if they are not totally trustworthy in relation to money, how can you trust them in relation to spiritual or pastoral matters?

Paul. The apostle Paul was very cautious about this matter of handling money. He made a collection of money among the Christian churches in Greece to take to the Jewish Christians in Jerusalem who were suffering great poverty and need. Paul talks about this collection a lot—in Romans 16, 1 Corinthians 16, and 2 Corinthians 8–9. It was clearly very important to him theologically as well as for its obvious practical purpose of meeting a need. Paul saw this gift of money as a real tangible proof that these Gentile believers had truly believed the gospel and were *obeying* it in sharing their material goods (which were not abundant—he says they were poor too) with the Jewish believers.

Now we might think that Paul could have simply said, "Just give me the money and I'll take it to Jerusalem. Trust me, I'm an apostle!" But no. Paul made sure that there were several other people beside himself involved in every aspect of the project, people who were trusted and appointed by the churches. These men would oversee the collection process and then travel along with Paul to make sure everything was honest and accounted for.

All the arrangements that Paul put in place were quite complicated (check them in 1 Cor 16:3-4; 2 Cor 8:16-24). It's not easy to identify all the people involved—except that it is clear there were several of them. It was also probably quite costly to carry out the whole operation in the way Paul arranged it. It would obviously cost a lot more for five or six men to travel from Greece to Jerusalem than for Paul to go there by himself; travel by land and sea was not cheap in those days any more than it is today.

So the arrangements and precautions that Paul built into the administration of this gift could have provoked resistance. People could have criticized and said, "Why send so many people? You are going to waste some of the gift on such expenses"—just as we sometimes complain about the cost of auditing our accounts. But Paul insists, "We want to avoid any criticism of the way we administer this liberal gift. *For we are taking pains to do what is right, not only in the eyes of the Lord but also in the eyes of man*" (2 Cor 8:20-21, emphasis mine).

Isn't that a wonderful statement? I think those verses should be a motto for faithfulness, honesty, and integrity. They should be hung on the wall of every Christian pastor, leader, and church or mission office.

Paul demanded full accountability—for himself and all those involved in the process of handling this money. Such accountability is a crucially important part of biblical integrity and faithfulness. Sadly, in many places it is glaringly absent, especially among Christian pastors and leaders who demand to be trusted and never to be questioned. But then, because they do not submit to the gift of accountability, they fall into temptation and their corruption brings disgrace on themselves and on the church, and on the name of Christ himself.

What is more, Paul applied this test of trustworthiness not only to himself and his companions, but even to slaves. Since slaves were so exploited and ill-treated, any slave might think that he owed his master nothing, so if he had the chance to cheat or steal from the master, why not? But Paul tells slaves who had become believers in Jesus that they must live with a different attitude. They should serve their masters as if serving the Lord himself (Eph 6:5-7), and that included being faithful and trustworthy (just as they would for the Lord). So he adds, "Teach slaves . . . to show that they can be fully trusted, so that in every way they will make the teaching about God our Savior attractive" (Titus 2:9-10).

In other words, faithfulness, honesty, and trustworthiness are qualities that commend the gospel to those who have not yet come to believe it.

A Final Thought

At the beginning of the chapter, we said that faithfulness also includes *long-term, steady, dependable, lifelong commitment.* Faithfulness in that sense includes loyalty, which means wholehearted, whole-life allegiance, born out of love and sustained by constant gratitude. That kind of commitment includes unwavering faithfulness to Christ himself, of course, as our Lord and Savior. It also means faithfulness to the Bible, faithfulness to the gospel, faithfulness to the church, and faithfulness to the work God has given you to do. It means faithfulness to the mission of God in the world and to all those who are engaged in it along with you.

Faithfulness means you know what you really *believe,* whom you really *love,* and what you are ultimately *committed* to. Faithfulness means being sure of what you want to live for and what you're willing to die for. Faithfulness is what author Eugene Peterson called "a long obedience in the same direction."

Paul loved to mention this kind of long-term, loyal faithfulness when he greeted people. He spoke about some of his companions as "faithful brothers"—that's a phrase that is used in various places about Timothy, Epaphras, Onesimus, Tychicus, and Apelles. And I'm sure Paul would have said the same about the women he mentions who, as he put it, "worked very hard in the Lord"—Phoebe, Priscilla, Mary, Junia, Tryphena, Tryphosa, and Persis. I love that list of people in Romans 16. It makes this whole issue very personal. These were *real* people—men and women, some of whom spent time in prison with Paul, and some who risked their lives for him. These were *faithful* friends—people Paul knew he could trust. And so Paul thanked God when he saw that fruit of the Spirit in their lives—their faithfulness to him and to their common mission.

In the same way, Peter commends Silas: "With the help of Silas, whom I regard as *a faithful brother,* I have written to you briefly, encouraging you and testifying that this is the true grace of God. Stand fast in it" (1 Pet 5:12, emphasis mine).

And the elder John commends Gaius for both his "faithfulness to the truth" and that he is being *"faithful in what [he is] doing* for the brothers and sisters" (3 Jn 3, 5). Clearly he was both a faithful preacher and a faithful pastor and supporter of others.

And so, at the end of his own long life, Paul could say those famous words:

> I have fought the good fight, I have finished the race, *I have kept the faith.* Now there is in store for me the crown of righteousness, which the Lord, the righteous Judge, will award to me on that day—and not only to me, but also to all who have longed for his appearing. (2 Tim 4:7-8, emphasis mine)

"Well done, good and faithful servant."

Questions

1. Study Bible characters who, like Moses, displayed the quality of faithfulness. Think, for example, of Joseph, Samuel, Elijah, Ruth, Daniel, Jeremiah, and others.

2. What Scripture passages help you reflect on the faithfulness of God? How do we reflect God's faithfulness in the way we live our own lives?

3. In what ways does your culture recognize and approve of faithfulness in human relationships? Does faithfulness as the fruit of the Spirit reflect such cultural values, or challenge them in any way?

4. Are there ways that Christians in your church or culture are tempted to *lack* faithfulness in their lives? In what way could you look to the Bible and learn to correct that?

Watch a video from Chris about faithfulness
at **ivpress.com/cultivating-faithfulness**.

8

GENTLENESS

Gentleness is very close to patience. It's not surprising to find them both included in Paul's list of the fruit of the Spirit. What's the similarity and difference?

Well, if patience is the ability to endure hostility and criticism *without anger,* then gentleness is the ability to endure such things without *aggression.* Gentleness shows itself when I've learned that the Christlike way to respond to conflicts and quarrels, rejection, unfairness, or harsh words spoken against me, is *not* with bluster and self-defense, *not* with harsh and aggressive words, *not* with angry gestures and facial expressions, *not* with prickles and spikes—but rather, with softness, controlling my tongue and my temper.

Gentleness means being very aware that the other person is a human being with feelings too. And maybe that person, even the one who is being very nasty, is just as hurt as I am by whatever is going on between us. So if I fight back with matching or increasing aggression, it will only make things worse. We will hurt each other even more, and what's the point in that?

Gentleness doesn't necessarily mean just saying nothing and soaking it up (though sometimes it might—think of Jesus at the time of his trial). A gentle response can also be strong, firm, and clear, but without vicious rage.

Gentleness is also very close to *humility,* and sometimes they come together. For example, they are the first things Paul mentions when he tells his readers to live lives that are worthy of their calling in the gospel. "As a prisoner for the Lord, then, I urge you to live a life worthy of the calling you have received. *Be completely humble and gentle;* be patient, bearing with one another in love" (Eph 4:1-2, emphasis mine).

Gentleness in the Ancient World

Now in the world of Greece and Rome—the world in which Paul was writing his letter to the Christians in Galatia—gentleness and humility were not highly valued at all. Aristotle did manage to include gentleness (the same Greek word that Paul uses here) in his lists of virtues. But it was a rather flimsy sort of virtue really.

Aristotle defined "gentleness" as "the golden mean" (that is, halfway) between two extremes. Gentleness, according to Aristotle, lies halfway between excessive anger (which is bad at one extreme), and being unable to get angry about anything at all—just being apathetic (which is also bad at the other extreme). Gentleness, for Aristotle, meant having a calmly measured response to everything life throws at you. So he thought gentleness in that sense was a good thing, or at least, it was better than throwing tantrums or not caring at all. But that makes it a rather negative thing—neither this nor that. That seems a long way from the positive, attractive gentleness that Paul envisages as the fruit of the Spirit of the living God, seen at its best in Jesus Christ.

Gentleness may have been a grudging sort of virtue for Aristotle, but humility (closely related to gentleness) was generally *despised* in the popular culture of Greece and Rome. Humility was not a virtue at all—it was emphatically *not* one of the heroic virtues. In fact humility was generally perceived as a vice. *Real men* were neither gentle nor humble. *Real men* were strong, powerful, and dominant. Boasting about your superiority was not regarded as being in bad taste in the way it is in modern polite society. Boasting was a carefully cultivated art form. Real men were winners! And real men made sure everybody else knew. So humility? No, no. If you had anything to boast about (and even if you hadn't), polish your boasting as best you can! *Don't* be humble! That was the surrounding culture of Paul's day.

That kind of supermasculine ideal still dominates much popular culture in Hollywood movies of the all-conquering, usually violent "good guy," and the mythical superheroes. Sadly, such machismo mentality seems very much alive at street level as well. Gentleness and humility? Who needs them? That's the way to get trampled on.

Those movies have a very powerful influence on us. To be honest, I have to confess that when I was a young lad I sometimes used to vaguely regret being a Christian when watching movies with powerful, manly heroes! Wouldn't it be great to be able to snap your fingers, say sharp and aggressive things, bark out the orders, and have people scurry off to do what you say? Or to pull out a gun, or be capable of all kinds of single combat techniques, and just blast the bad guys out of sight? But as a Christian I knew I couldn't do any of those things— or at least, I knew that I *shouldn't* do them even if I could. Being gentle and humble doesn't seem like half as much fun!

So subtly and dangerously, the culture and its heroes shape our thinking and attitudes. And sadly even some Christian leaders fall into the temptation of being the kind of "superhero" leaders that popular culture imagines. There are some pastors and some presidents of Christian organizations who behave in autocratic ways, demanding instant compliance with their instructions. Gentleness and humility— the very characteristics of Christ—are far from their personality, words, and actions. As a result, they actually become quite un-Christlike, even as Christian leaders.

But the Bible presents a very different ideal—one that was countercultural then, and still is today. Paul's list of the fruit of the Spirit included terms that would have been surprising to his contemporaries. In fact, it is only the power and influence of the Christian gospel (along with the presence of the Holy Spirit, of course) that has created the perception and acceptance of gentleness and humility as virtues at all (even within secular society). Ultimately, of course, it is because of the character of Christ himself—who modeled the incredible strength of true gentleness and humility—that led to this slow transformation of a cultural norm. By the power of the gospel and the attractive witness of generations of believers in whom the fruit of the Spirit was seen, something that had once been seen as shameful, weak, and despised, came to be regarded as among the primary and most Christlike virtues of all—gentleness and humility.

As before, we need to start with God. And once again, surprising though it seems, we need to start in the Old Testament.

The Gentleness of God in the Old Testament

Gentleness is probably not the first thing you'd think of to describe God in the Old Testament. Yet the psalmists and others often speak of God in gentle terms. Of course, they also speak of his incredible power—mighty like the storm, with a voice to melt the mountains. Yes, but they use other metaphors too.

David compares God to the gentle shepherd caring for the needs of his sheep, leading them to calm water for drinking, fresh pasture for feeding, and protecting them through the place of danger.

> He makes me lie down in green pastures,
> he leads me beside quiet waters,
>   he refreshes my soul.
> He guides me along the right paths
>   for his name's sake. (Ps 23:2-3)

Isaiah develops the same picture. After describing God's almighty power, Isaiah goes on:

He tends his flock like a shepherd:
> He gathers the lambs in his arms
and carries them close to his heart;
> he gently leads those that have young. (Is 40:11)

God is gentle like a parent who knows that his children are weak and vulnerable:

As a father has compassion on his children,
> so the LORD has compassion on those who fear him;
for he knows how we are formed,
> he remembers that we are dust. (Ps 103:13-14)

Deuteronomy pictures God as a caring father. He carries his people as a father carries his children, to keep them out of danger. Of course, the parental picture includes discipline as well, but carried out within the context of gentle provision for all our needs.

There [in the wilderness] you saw how the LORD your God carried you, *as a father carries his son*, all the way you went until you reached this place. (Deut 1:31, emphasis mine)

Remember how the LORD your God led you all the way in the wilderness these forty years, to humble and test you in order to know what was in your heart, whether or not you would keep his commands. He humbled you, causing you to hunger and then feeding you with manna, which neither you nor your ancestors had known, to teach you that man does not live on bread alone but on every word that comes from the mouth of the LORD. Your clothes did not wear out and your feet did not swell during these forty years. Know then in your heart that *as a man disciplines his son*, so the LORD your God disciplines you. (Deut 8:2-5, emphasis mine)

And then there are some stories that portray God dealing with people tenderly—which we easily forget when we only recall the stories of his anger and judgment.

Think of Hagar. When Hagar first fled from Abraham and Sarah (in Gen 16) because Sarah was abusing her, Hagar was wandering in the wilderness, pregnant but facing certain death. Who found her? Not the gods of Egypt where she had come from and was probably trying to get back to, but the God of Abraham himself. And after God had given her comfort and a promise about the son she would bear, she became the first person in the Bible to give a name to God—"You are El Roi," she said, "the God who sees me" (Gen 16:13). A foreign, slave, concubine woman! That was the gentleness of God for Hagar, and it happened again, when she was actually thrown out by Abraham with her young son Ishmael. The second time (Gen 21:8-21), God saved both their lives, providing water in the wilderness (something God is rather good at doing).

Think of Elijah. I love the gentle way God dealt with Elijah when he was feeling depressed and suicidal, and running for his life from the threats of Jezebel (in 1 Kings 19). When God found Elijah in the desert, sheltering under a juniper tree and wanting to die, God cared for him, giving him sleep and food. And what food—bread freshly baked in heaven and delivered by an angel! God's gentleness is astonishing in that story (though we don't hear that Elijah even said thank you for the food! He just ate it and went back to sleep).

Then God took him back to Mount Sinai and gave him a great audiovisual demonstration of wind, earthquake, and fire. But significantly, "The LORD was not in the wind . . . not in the earthquake . . . not in the fire" (1 Kings 19:11-12). So how then did God speak to Elijah? Through "a gentle whisper," or in the older translations, "a still small voice." God was *gentle* with his failing prophet. And then he restored him and sent him back to his mission. This was divine gentleness at work. I think it is a prefiguring of the way Jesus dealt with Peter, which we'll address below.

The Gentleness of Jesus

"Gentle Jesus, meek and mild / thou wast once a little child."

Some of us (of a certain age) may remember that old children's hymn. But when we use that language about Jesus, it doesn't mean that he was a wimp who never raised his voice or stood up to others. On the contrary, Jesus could speak the truth very boldly and confront people with great strength. The Gospels have plenty of illustrations of that. But his greatest strength was best seen in his gentleness. Jesus did not get aggressive or belligerent when his enemies tried to trick him and even when they falsely accused him. Jesus did not bully or belittle others, and he made time for those whom the rest of society *did* bully, belittle, and reject.

One of the best-loved sayings of Jesus is: "Come to me, all you who are weary and burdened, and I will give you rest. Take my yoke upon you and learn from me, *for I am gentle and humble in heart,* and you will find rest for your souls" (Mt 11:28-29, emphasis mine).

In speaking of his "yoke," Jesus was contrasting his own way with the way of the teachers of the Mosaic law. There was an expression: "Taking upon yourself the yoke of the law." It meant that the faithful Israelite should bend his neck and submit to the law of the Lord, as an ox does to the yoke the farmer puts on him. And there is a sense, of course, in which that is very right and good. God gave Israel his law so that, if they would obey it and submit to his covenant authority, it would be best for them. The law was given to the people after God had redeemed them as a way of enabling them to live within the sphere of that blessing of redemption. Their society and culture would be filled with integrity, justice, and compassion. So submitting to the yoke of the law was intended to be a positive, wholesome, and life-giving thing to do.

But by the time of Jesus, the guardians of Israelite society—the Pharisees and scribes, the people who studied, taught, and tried to enforce the law—had added so much to the law that it had become a wearisome burden. Far from freeing people to enjoy their relationship with God, it had become an instrument of crushing conformity. It was anything but "gentle," and those public leaders were anything but "humble."

Well, Jesus certainly did not call people to *throw off* the yoke of the law—meaning the Scriptures of the Torah itself. Throwing off the yoke of the law was one way that the prophets had described Israel's rebellious nature in the Old Testament era (e.g., Jer 2:20). It meant being disobedient to God and refusing to submit to his authority, which Israel had done for centuries. No, Jesus was insistent—he had not come to *abolish* the law and the prophets, but rather to *fulfill* them. People needed to see *him*, Jesus, as their perfect teacher, leader, and model. They needed to see him as the true embodiment of what the law really aimed at—a loving, faithful, compassionate, and obedient relationship with God. And they could live that way if they would take *his* "yoke" upon themselves and submit to him.

Discipleship of Jesus, following Jesus, means becoming more and more like him—that is, being characterized by the gentleness and humility of Christ himself. And that kind of Christlikeness, the fruit of the Spirit of Jesus, is so different from the harshness and arrogance that can easily poison and pollute the way some people behave when their religion becomes self-righteously confrontational. The following are some outstanding examples of the gentleness of Jesus in the Gospel stories.

The Samaritan woman. When Jesus spoke to the Samaritan woman at the well in John 4, it was astonishingly gentle, even though it was also direct and truthful. When he tells her she has had five husbands, we often hear his words as a rebuke, or as implying that she was a degraded, promiscuous woman. But while she accepts that it was true, it need not have been due to her own unfaithfulness. Divorce was the man's prerogative in that culture, so she might just as easily have been the victim of male exploitation—used and thrown away by five callous men and now living with a man in an unmarried state. We really can't tell from the text what circumstances had led to her five broken marriages, but whatever they were, Jesus leads her gently to acknowledge her greatest need—the living water from God's Messiah and a right relationship with God "in the Spirit and in truth" (Jn 4:23) through Jesus. The fact that he was speaking to her at all, let alone the fact that it was such a gentle, respectful conversation, was a shock to the returning disciples.

The Syro-Phoenician woman. Even less acceptable to the culture than a Samaritan woman was the Syro-Phoenician woman in Mark 7.

> Jesus left that place and went to the vicinity of Tyre. He entered a house and did not want anyone to know it; yet he could not keep his presence secret. In fact, as soon as she heard about him, a woman whose little daughter was possessed by an impure spirit came and fell at his feet. The woman was a Greek, born in Syrian Phoenicia. She begged Jesus to drive the demon out of her daughter. (Mk 7:24-26)

We don't know in advance exactly why Jesus went to that Gentile region, though by the time the story ends, we may well assume that it was precisely so that someone such as that lady could be brought by faith into the blessing of the kingdom of God through Jesus.

At first, of course, the way Jesus responded to her request to come and heal her daughter sounds anything but gentle. "First let the children eat all they want," he told her, "for it is not right to take the children's bread and toss it to the dogs" (Mk 7:27).

But part of the problem is that we can only read his words; we can't hear the tone of his voice, or the look in his eye. I rather imagine (nothing more than that), that Jesus spoke with the kind of twinkle in his eye which communicated to the woman something like, "You know I have to say something like this, me being a Jew and you being a Gentile, but are you going to be content with it as an answer, or will you push back at me?"

And the woman takes the hint, and replies with a brilliant piece of proverbial logic: "'Lord,' she replied, 'even the dogs under the table eat the children's crumbs'" (Mk 7:28). What she means is, "Even if, as you say, the Jews here with you think of me as a Gentile dog, don't dogs get scraps from the good food on the table for the children? Why then can't I, a Gentile, benefit from what you, the Messiah, are doing for the Jews?"

And of course, her feisty sharp wit actually fits precisely with the whole theological thrust of the Old Testament Scriptures (not that she would have known that). For that was exactly what God had indeed promised. God had created Israel precisely so that the rest of the nations would benefit. Blessing for Israel meant blessing for the nations of the world. For that very purpose Christ had come. Without knowing those Scriptures of Israel, this woman has a perfectly accurate intuition of God's intention for Israel and through Israel for the Gentiles.

So, in my view, Jesus' apparently sharp words are part of a gentle probing that draws out the woman's faith into open view. And as soon as Jesus recognizes her faith, he immediately responds according to her request. She went home and found that the demon had left her daughter, who was now lying peacefully on her bed.

Jesus' arrest, trial, and crucifixion. The gentleness of Jesus was tested most severely, of course, through his arrest, trial, and crucifixion. When he was arrested, he could have called on twelve legions of angels to protect him, but he didn't (Mt 26:53-54). When he was facing trials, before the Jewish court and then the Roman one, he could have answered every charge with angry rebuttal, but he remained mostly silent (Mt 26:63). When they were nailing him to the cross, he could have called down curses on his enemies (as Jeremiah, some psalmists, and some of the Maccabean martyrs did). But he didn't; he prayed to his Father to forgive them (Lk 23:34). And in the midst of his agony on the cross, he thought of the needs of his mother and entrusted her to the care of one of his disciples (Jn 19:26-27).

No wonder Peter later saw in that whole story of the trial and crucifixion of Jesus an enactment of the response of the Servant of the Lord to his executioners, quoting from Isaiah 53.

> But if you suffer for doing good and you endure it, this is commendable before God. To this you were called, because Christ suffered for you, leaving you an example, that you should follow in his steps.
>
> "He committed no sin,
>   and no deceit was found in his mouth."
>
> When they hurled their insults at him, he did not retaliate; when he suffered, he made no threats. Instead, he entrusted himself to him who judges justly. (1 Pet 2:20-23)

Peter's restoration. And finally, after the resurrection, think of the gentle way Jesus restored Peter after his appalling failure. Peter had denied Jesus three times, which must have led to unbearable grief, guilt, and remorse. Peter quite probably thought that his days as a trusted disciple of Jesus and leader of the team were over, with no hope of reprieve or restoration. How could he ever face Jesus again? How, indeed, did Peter ever face the other disciples again when they heard what he had done?

Did such questions and accusations hang in the air with the smoke of the fire during that breakfast time by the lake when the risen Jesus baked bread and fish for the hungry disciples (Jn 21)? Almost certainly. And why is it that John alone of the Gospel writers tells us this story of what Jesus said to Peter that morning? I am convinced that John records this moment between Jesus and Peter because John had been there when Peter denied Jesus!

It is John who tells us that the only reason why Peter had been able to get access to that courtyard where Jesus was on trial was because there was "another disciple" who had friends on the inside who let him in. Almost certainly that "other disciple" was John himself (Jn 18:15-16).

So John, unbelievably, would have heard those shocking denials by Peter that he was one of the followers of Jesus. John had heard his closest friend, with whom he had shared the most intimate moments with Jesus over the past three years, shouting out that he didn't even know the man! Three times he did it! Possibly even cursing Jesus! The text says simply that Peter called down curses. Most English translations add the words, "on himself." But I imagine it's quite possible Peter went so far as to say, "I don't know this Jesus of Nazareth, curse him!" How could John ever trust Peter again? How could Peter ever preach or teach about Jesus (with John listening) after that?

So it is John who tells us that *three times*, after breakfast on the shore of the lake, the risen Jesus asked Peter, "Do you love me?" (Jn 21:15-17). That was tough—the three questions obviously recalling the three denials. Excruciatingly tough, yes, but it was also gentle.

Jesus did not rebuke Peter, or shame him in the presence of the other disciples. In fact, it seems that Jesus did not ask those questions publicly. John records that after Jesus had asked the questions, and Peter had answered them, Peter turned around and saw John following—and presumably listening. In other words, the conversation probably happened on foot, not still sitting around the fire with everybody else. It seems that this was after the breakfast was over, and Jesus and Peter were walking away from the lake talking together privately. But John, following just behind, most likely overhears the conversation. John hears Peter say, three times, in anguished repentance but in passionate sincerity, that he truly loves Jesus. And that was all Jesus needed to know, and that was all John needed to hear. And that is probably why John alone records it.

So Peter the failure became Peter the forgiven—through the gentleness of Jesus. And judging from the Peter we next meet in the book of Acts on the day of Pentecost and beyond, that gentle restoration by Jesus was effective. Peter himself would have been a man of gentleness and humility after that, for sure.

Gentleness as the Christian Way of Life

So with all these teachings and examples of Jesus, it's not surprising that Paul turned gentleness and humility from being despised qualities in his surrounding culture into prime evidence of the work of the Spirit of Jesus in our lives. The very things the world *mocked*, Paul affirmed as qualities that make us *more like Christ*.

Paul modeled it himself. He had some pretty tough things to say to the church at Corinth, but he began this way, "By the humility and *gentleness* of Christ, I appeal to you . . ." (2 Cor 10:1, emphasis mine). When you read the rest of that chapter, you may wonder, "If that's Paul being gentle, what must he have been like when he was fierce?!" Still, it shows that Paul was not a bullying church leader. He longed for healed relationships and spiritual restoration, and he saw gentleness as the key to that goal—starting with his own gentleness as a model.

Then Paul tells other Christians to follow his example, whenever there is failure in the lives of other believers. "Brothers and sisters, if someone is caught in a sin, you who live by the Spirit should restore that person *gently*" (Gal 6:1, emphasis mine).

If only that were the regular normal practice in our churches and Christian organizations! Sadly, when someone falls down in some way, it is more likely they will be judged and rejected, rather than gently restored. There is a place for appropriate church discipline (though it is a terribly difficult area for any church in practice). But whatever form that discipline takes, Paul says it must be done in gentleness. Those who are filled with the Spirit (or who claim to be), must demonstrate the fruit of the Spirit, including gentleness, in dealing with those who fail or fall—just as Jesus himself did.

Paul makes this a particular command for those who are in church leadership—where it is needed so badly. "The Lord's servant must not be quarrelsome but must be kind to everyone, able to teach, not resentful. Opponents must be *gently* instructed, in the hope that God

will grant them repentance leading them to a knowledge of the truth"
(2 Tim 2:24-25, emphasis mine).

How very different is that from the way some Christian leaders
behave? And what about those who write comments on other people's
blogs? So often these are quarrelsome, unkind, and resentful. And yet,
unless pastors and leaders set an example of such gentleness, how can
we expect the rest of God's people to be like that?

Paul went further and turned this quality of gentleness into a
general principle that should govern all our relationships—it's not just
for leaders. Here's what Paul told Titus to teach his people: "Remind
the people to . . . be ready to do whatever is good, to slander no one,
to be peaceable and considerate, and *always to be gentle toward everyone*" (Titus 3:1-2, emphasis mine).

Sadly, many of us, including some outspoken Christian leaders,
need a lot of reminding of that. When you think of the most outspoken, most blogged, most celebrated, most published, most followed
church leaders of your country or culture, would *gentleness* be among
the most noticeable things about them that spring to your mind?

Peter, who must have often remembered how gently Jesus dealt
with him, tells us that this should be an important quality of the way
we speak to people who are not yet Christians, perhaps especially
when we are engaging with people of other faiths. "Always be prepared
to give an answer to everyone who asks you to give the reason for the
hope you have. *But do this with gentleness and respect*" (1 Pet 3:15, emphasis mine).

Again, it needs to be asked: Is this characteristic of the way Christians engage in evangelistic encounters? And when you think of the
way Christians in your culture respond to criticism or challenges or
persecution or mockery, would you put gentleness and respect high up
on the list of the ways they speak and behave?

Where does this kind of gentleness come from? Well, we might
reply, it is the fruit of the Spirit. Yes indeed. It is the character of Jesus

living within us. But I think that in practical day-to-day terms, the deepest root of this kind of gentleness is genuine humility. And by humility I mean the deep awareness that I am just as human and flawed and tempted as anyone else. I really have no reason to feel superior and get aggressive when other people show their flaws and failings. Not if I know my own heart.

So when somebody else makes a mistake, or drops something, or loses the keys, or forgets to do what they promised, or generally messes things up—things that happen to all of us at some point in life—at that moment I try not to lose my temper and rage at them, shouting angry words of accusation and blame. No, I control that instinctive response, because I remind myself (often just in time) that it could just as easily have been *me* making that mistake. And if it had been me, how would I want others to respond to my foolishness or weakness or mistakes?

Humility comes a lot easier when you really know yourself, when you know the weak and flawed person who is living inside the shell you have on the outside. Then, out of that deep well of self-knowledge and gratitude for the grace of God that has rescued you from your own sin and failure, comes *humility before God* and *gentleness towards others*.

If God has been gentle and gracious to me, and if I would like other people to be gentle with me when I mess up, then let me pray to be like that to them. As a forgiven sinner myself, let me welcome others to the fellowship of the forgiven. Let the gentle fruit of the Spirit ripen in my life and relationships.

Questions

1. What other examples of the gentleness of Jesus in action could you add to the ones described in the chapter above?

2. What are the reasons why people are so often *not* gentle toward others? When do you personally find it most difficult to exercise gentleness to others, and why?

3. If one reason is that many cultures expect people in positions of authority and leadership to be strong and assertive (not humble and gentle), how can Christian leaders learn to exercise their leadership with humility and gentleness?

4. The gentleness of God is described by using the metaphors of a shepherd and a loving parent. How can these pictures help in working out what it means to exercise gentleness in our own lives that reflect the gentleness of God?

Watch a video from Chris about gentleness
at **ivpress.com/cultivating-gentleness**.

SELF-CONTROL

We come to the last on Paul's list of the fruit of the Spirit—self-control. This word throws us back sharply to that horrible list of "the works of the flesh" that comes immediately before the fruit of the Spirit.

> The acts of the flesh are obvious: sexual immorality, impurity and debauchery; idolatry and witchcraft; hatred, discord, jealousy, fits of rage, selfish ambition, dissensions, factions and envy; drunkenness, orgies, and the like. I warn you, as I did before, that those who live like this will not inherit the kingdom of God. (Gal 5:19-21)

Many of the behaviors that Paul lists show human nature *out of control* and at its sinful, excessive worst. That kind of uncontrolled life lets people give in to self-indulgence, sexual gratification, pride, gluttony, and so on. Self-control is the opposite of those kinds of sinful behaviors.

That fact is probably the reason why self-control is the one and only fruit of the Spirit for which we don't have a matching quality of God. For God does not need to exercise self-control over any sinful tendency within himself. God does not have to hold in check any evil desires. "God is light; in him there is no darkness at all," as John said

(1 Jn 1:5). God is not tempted in any way by evil. So in that sense (self-control over evil desires), this is not a quality of God.

In each chapter so far, we have looked at all the other items in Paul's list of the fruit of the Spirit, and we have seen how each one reflects something of God. We can quickly think of Bible teaching about the love of God, the joy of the Lord, the peace of God, as well as God's patience, kindness, goodness, faithfulness, and gentleness. But when we come to this last item, we have to admit that self-control is something *we* need—not something *God* has to exercise.

Why then is it included in a list of the fruit of the Spirit? Surely it is because one of the things that the Holy Spirit does within us is that he enables and empowers us to control our sinful desires. This does not mean that, in this earthly life, we achieve perfection and never fall or fail. But it does mean that we remember, as Paul taught us, that our bodies are temples of the Holy Spirit and so we ask the resident Holy Spirit to control us so that we learn to control ourselves. We will look in the conclusion at how Paul explains further what he means by keeping "in step with the Spirit" (Gal 5:25).

There is a similar list to Paul's fruit of the Spirit in the opening verses of 2 Peter. There, self-control is among the qualities that we should seek to add to our faith, in response to God's divine power and promises, as we grow to maturity and effectiveness in our relationship with Christ.

> For this very reason, make every effort to add to your faith goodness; and to goodness, knowledge; and to knowledge, *self-control*; and to self-control, perseverance; and to perseverance, godliness; and to godliness, mutual affection; and to mutual affection, love. For if you possess these qualities in increasing measure, they will keep you from being ineffective and unproductive in your knowledge of our Lord Jesus Christ. But whoever does not have them is nearsighted and blind, forgetting that they have been cleansed from their past sins. (2 Pet 1:5-9, emphasis mine)

Earlier we saw that Aristotle did not have much positive to say about the virtue of gentleness, and that the closely linked quality of humility was not regarded as a virtue at all in the world of ancient Greece and Rome. However, in his extensive writing on virtues and ethics, Aristotle did praise this one—self-control (using the same word as Paul does in Gal 5:23). For Aristotle, the word meant the ability to have powerful passions, but to keep them under control. The virtuous person can think and feel very strongly about things, and have real passions. But the virtue lies in keeping control of them, so that all the energy of one's passions serves good ends, and doesn't lead to selfish or destructive results.

Aristotle probably would have agreed with the message of a big roadside ad that I once saw in Uganda. It was an ad for tires that filled a massive billboard. There was a striking (and somewhat threatening) picture of a huge fist coming right at your face, knuckles downwards, bursting out of the background almost three-dimensionally. But at the bottom of the picture, the knuckles of the fist morphed into the shape of four massive tires—the kind of enormous tires with deep treads that you see on giant road trucks. The message below the picture read: "Power is nothing without control." You can have massive power and energy coming from the engine of the truck. But unless it is kept under control "where the rubber hits the road," things can be very dangerous indeed. Power has to be controlled for it to be safe.

And Paul would have agreed with Aristotle. We do indeed have powerful drives and passions that need to be kept under control. But since some of our passions are part of our fallen, sinful nature, how can they be controlled? We do not have the ability in ourselves to do so successfully in our own strength. We can try to exercise self-control, in the same way that Aristotle commended us to cultivate it as a virtue. But Aristotle did not take into account the nature of sin.

Sin has a power of its own operating against our best intentions, and it very quickly gets out of control and carries us along with it. Paul, on the other hand, knew only too well about the power of sin and the flesh, and he knew that the only power sufficient to keep it under control is the Holy Spirit. So he adds this final piece of the Spirit's fruit. Part of the work of the Holy Spirit within us is the way he enables us to keep the sinful desires and impulses that still lurk within us under control. Self-control does involve effort of the will, but it is an effort inspired and empowered by the Spirit of God as his will bears fruit in our will.

Probably the main thing (but certainly not the only thing) that Paul has in mind as regards what we need to control is our sexual desires. Certainly, his list of "the works of the flesh" begins with sexual immorality, and in several other places Paul includes that among his lists of sinful behavior that Christians should put aside altogether (e.g., 1 Cor 5:9-11; Eph 5:3-7; Col 3:5-10).

If we could have asked Paul for examples from the Scriptures, I think he might have mentioned Joseph. Joseph had been put in charge of all the affairs of his master, Potiphar, in Egypt. He rose to prominence and success, though still technically a slave. He had reached the point where many men in his position felt free to take sexual liberties as their due reward. And that temptation came his way, not with a slave-girl, but with Potiphar's wife.

> Now Joseph was well-built and handsome, and after a while his master's wife took notice of Joseph and said, "Come to bed with me!"
>
> But he refused. "With me in charge," he told her, "my master does not concern himself with anything in the house; everything he owns he has entrusted to my care. No one is greater in this house than I am. My master has withheld nothing from me except you, because you are his wife. How then could I do such a wicked thing and sin against God?" And though she spoke to Joseph day after day, he refused to go to bed with her or even to be with her.

One day he went into the house to attend to his duties, and none of the household servants was inside. She caught him by his cloak and said, "Come to bed with me!" But he left his cloak in her hand and ran out of the house. (Gen 39:6-12)

In that little story we can see not only Joseph's self-control, but also the powerful reasons he gives for it. The first is that he was not willing to break the trust of his master (he could also stand as an example of faithfulness for that reason). But even more, he was not willing to sin against God. Now the author of Genesis has told us several times that God was with Joseph in all the ups and downs of his life. So we might even suggest that the fruit of the Spirit is being modeled by Joseph at this point, for his self-control was not just a matter of his own strength, but his awareness of God in his life.

As a counterexample we might think of the much longer, and much sadder, story of David. His lack of self-control after seeing Bathsheba bathing led him not only into adultery but also into a deepening morass of deception and planned murder. And even though he repented and experienced God's forgiveness, his loss of personal self-control meant that he also lost moral control over his own family—especially two of his sons, Amnon and Absalom—who amplified their father's sexual sins to their own eventual destruction (the whole sorry tale fills 2 Sam 11–17).

Temptation to sexual activity and relations outside the good context God provided for sex (within marriage) remains very strong and is a powerful enemy for any of us at any age. We need to recognize what a dangerous enemy it is, whether in actual practice, or in the world of our thoughts and imagination, through pornography and other sources. Of course sexual temptation targets both men and women, but there seems little doubt that it is particularly potent in men (and as a man, I'm allowed to say that, for I know it to be true).

The stupendous scale of human suffering caused by uncontrolled male lust and sexual anarchy is beyond imagination. Uncountable numbers of women and little girls and boys all over the world suffer at the hands of rapists, pimps, sex-traffickers, pedophiles, abusers, violent husbands, and plain, ordinary adulterers. Such things were present in Paul's day also, though perhaps not on the scale we have come to witness in the modern world. So Paul is taking a strongly countercultural stance when he tells Christians that they must have nothing to do with such practices, ever. And the only way to do that is through the Spirit-empowered exercise of self-control.

Those of us who are in any form of Christian leadership—pastors, missionaries, youth workers, or theological teachers—need to heed Paul's teaching here more than most. For somehow, with depressing frequency, the evil one manages to seduce precisely such people into sexual sin, sometimes to the destruction of whatever ministry God had entrusted to them. Of course there is grace and forgiveness whenever there is true repentance. We know the cleansing power of the blood of Christ and the amazing redemptive, restorative truth of the gospel. But the damage done may be irreversible at a human level, and the damage done to the name of Christ in the world is a grievous pain to God and a shame on the church. And so often, sadly so very often, the worst scandals begin with a momentary loss of self-control, or with the slow failure over time to exercise self-control over one's eyes and imagination, until the longed for but unthinkable deed becomes available and then actual.

But perhaps we have reached a place in our lives where we think we have that particular form of temptation (sexual immorality) well under control. Maybe our circumstances in life and ministry are very unlikely to provide either the temptation or the opportunity to fall into sexual sin. Well, apart from the warning, "If you think you are standing firm, be careful that you don't fall!" (1 Cor 10:12), Paul's list reminds us that "the flesh," our fallen human nature, has plenty of other desires and tendencies, bad habits, traps, and temptations for us to fall into if we don't exercise self-control with the help of the Spirit. Take a look at that list at the start of the chapter again.

Paul begins with *sexual immorality* and ends with *orgies*. Maybe you can't imagine even knowing where to find an orgy, let alone having the energy to join in. But are you in control of your *temper*? Paul includes *fits of rage* in his list. I know of some senior Christian leaders who are notorious for getting very angry with others, shouting at their staff, and so on. Where is their self-control in those moments?

And what about your *appetite*? Is that under control? We can all enjoy good food that God provides as a blessing to be received with thanksgiving. But *drunkenness* and *gluttony* are among the sins the Bible condemns.

Are you in control of your *attitude* toward others? When others do well or get what you would like for yourself, can you control the urge to *jealousy* and *envy* and *selfish ambition*?

Are you in control of your *time* (insofar as you are able), or wasting a lot of it in laziness or lack of self-discipline?

Are you in control of what is perhaps the hardest thing of all to exercise self-control over—your *tongue*? Paul does not list that specifically here (though it would be involved in *discord* and *dissensions*), but he would certainly have agreed with the way James stressed the damage the tongue can do and the need to control it severely.

When we put bits into the mouths of horses to make them obey us, we can turn the whole animal. Or take ships as an example. Although they are so large and are driven by strong winds, they are steered by a very small rudder wherever the pilot wants to go. Likewise, the tongue is a small part of the body, but it makes great boasts. Consider what a great forest is set on fire by a small spark. The tongue also is a fire, a world of evil among the parts of the body. It corrupts the whole body, sets the whole course of one's life on fire, and is itself set on fire by hell.

All kinds of animals, birds, reptiles and sea creatures are being tamed and have been tamed by mankind, but no human being can tame the tongue. It is a restless evil, full of deadly poison.

With the tongue we praise our Lord and Father, and with it we curse human beings, who have been made in God's likeness. Out of the same mouth come praise and cursing. My brothers and sisters, this should not be. (Jas 3:3-10)

"This should not be," James says. But sadly, it often is. Lack of self-control in the use of our tongues is a huge cause of damage in Christian fellowship. And that can apply not only to what we say with our mouths, but also what we write in emails, blogs, or comments. The language that some Christians use with each other and about each other is simply shameful at times. The evidence of the fruit of the Spirit in the exercise of self-control is sorely needed in the world of Christian communication.

Since speaking and writing are among the activities of Christian leaders, it is not surprising that Paul emphasizes self-control as an essential criterion for Christian leaders (those he calls elders and overseers).

Since an overseer manages God's household, he must be blameless—not overbearing, not quick-tempered, not given to drunkenness, not violent, not pursuing dishonest gain. Rather, he must be hospitable, one who loves what is good, who is *self-controlled*, upright, holy and disciplined. (Titus 1:7-8, emphasis mine)

After all, if someone cannot control themselves, their own words and actions, how can they be trusted to exercise any kind of appropriate and godly "control" in the church?

And just in case those of us who may be older imagine that it is particularly the youth who need to exercise self-control, look at Titus 2:2-8 and notice how many times, and to which groups of people, Paul speaks about self-control. The Greek word Paul uses in Titus, translated "self-controlled," is different from the one at the end of the fruit of the Spirit, but it has a very similar meaning.

Teach the older men to be temperate, worthy of respect, *self-controlled*, and sound in faith, in love and in endurance.

Likewise, teach the older women to be reverent in the way they live, not to be slanderers or addicted to much wine, but to teach what is good. Then they can urge the younger women to love their husbands and children, to be *self-controlled* and pure, to be busy at home, to be kind, and to be subject to their husbands, so that no one will malign the word of God.

Similarly, encourage the young men to be *self-controlled*. In everything set them an example by doing what is good. In your teaching show integrity, seriousness and soundness of speech that cannot be condemned, so that those who oppose you may be ashamed because they have nothing bad to say about us. (Titus 2:2-8, emphasis mine)

Paul does not see self-control as something especially needed by the young. No, he wisely says that it is something that needs to be taught and practiced by *all ages*—young and old, and by *both genders*—men and women. It is something for the whole church, just like the rest of the fruit of the Spirit.

So Paul has come full circle in his portrayal of the fruit of the Spirit. He began with love, which is a quality that directs our thoughts and actions outward toward others. And he ends with self-control, which is a quality that directs our thoughts and actions inward toward ourselves for our own good and that of others. And probably, Paul has in mind that unless we exercise this somewhat negative but necessary practice of self-control and live in a disciplined way (a way disciplined by the *Holy* Spirit), we will not be likely to bear the rest of the fruit of the Spirit.

Questions

1. What are the typical forms of lack of self-control that are evident in your culture? In what ways are Christians also tempted in the same way?

2. Where, in your own life, do you see the need for greater self-control? What steps will you take, spiritually and in practice, to cultivate this part of the fruit of the Spirit?

3. What are practical ways in which you could, by example, carry out what Paul tells Titus to do in the passage above (Titus 2:2-8)?

Watch a video from Chris about self-control
at **ivpress.com/cultivating-self-control**.

CONCLUSION

So we come to the end of our study of the wonderful qualities in Paul's list of the fruit of the Spirit. We began, in the introduction, by reminding ourselves that God's longing for every Christian believer is that they should become more and more like Jesus. And one of the key ways toward that kind of Christlikeness is to cultivate the fruit of the Spirit.

We read that John Stott prayed every day that God would make the fruit of the Spirit ripen in his life. And as God answered that prayer, Stott's life and character unself-consciously modeled Christlikeness among all who knew him. Stott's great ambition, which shaped the ongoing vision of Langham Partnership that he founded, was that Christians and churches around the world should be transformed by growing in maturity and Christlikeness so that they would be more effective in their mission in the world.

Stott went on to insist that spiritual maturity and Christlikeness are not only the fruit of the Spirit, but also the fruit of the Word of God as it takes deep root in our lives. Indeed, since the Holy Spirit inspired the Scriptures, it is very natural that he should use the Scriptures to bring to life and ripeness the fruit that he wants to see in us.

So the concluding message of this book has to be this: let's get back to the Bible in daily study and in faithful preaching, if preaching is our calling from God. We must not isolate the two verses in which Paul lists the fruit of the Spirit from the rest of their context.

In the introduction, we explored the background and setting of Paul's letter to the believers in Galatia. Now, in our conclusion, we need to finish off by returning to our text and observing three things that Paul says immediately after his list of the fruit of the Spirit. Here are the key verses again:

> The fruit of the Spirit is love, joy, peace, patience, kindness, goodness, faithfulness, gentleness and self-control. Against such things there is no law. Those who belong to Christ Jesus have crucified the sinful nature with its passions and desires. Since we live by the Spirit, let us keep in step with the Spirit. (Gal 5:22-25 NIV 1984)

"Against Such Things There Is No Law" (Gal 5:23)

This seems a very odd statement that Paul makes at the very end of his list. We might feel like exclaiming, "Well, of course not! You don't pass laws against kindness! There are no laws prohibiting love, joy, and peace!" So what does Paul mean here? Is he just stating the obvious, something nobody would disagree with?

It seems very probable that Paul is quoting a proverbial saying that goes back to Aristotle (who, as we've mentioned a few times, wrote a lot about ethics and virtues). In one place, after Aristotle had discussed a whole list of different qualities of a virtuous man, he wrote exactly the same Greek words that Paul uses here (which is why scholars think that Paul is intentionally quoting him, like a proverb). And many commentators think that the word that our Bible translates as "against" (the Greek word *kata*) would be better translated "concerning," or "in relation to."

In other words, what Paul (and Aristotle) meant was something like this: "In relation to these things, there is no law." *The New English*

Bible translates Galatians 5:23 as "there is no law dealing with such things as these." That is, these qualities are character virtues; you can't legislate to make people behave this way. People will do these things because of who they are, not because there are laws that compel them to. The law is not really relevant here.

So Paul, in his complex discussion of the law (of Moses) and the Spirit, is saying in effect, "Here are some characteristic qualities that the Holy Spirit will produce like fruit in your life as he lives within you. These things are not like legislation. This kind of life is not a matter of law at all. This kind of Christlike character does not come from submitting to the *law*, but from submitting to *Christ* by faith, and living your life under the power and guidance of his *Spirit*."

So, as we said right at the start, the fruit of the Spirit is a matter of *character*. The kind of attitudes and behaviors that Paul lists come not from the rules you keep, but from *the person you are*. Or rather, to be more specific, this way of living flows from *the person you are becoming* as you become more and more like Christ. Or, to be more specific still, such behavior flows from *the Person who dwells within you*, as Christ is formed in you (remember Gal 4:19) and the Spirit of Christ bears his fruit in your life.

And that point (that this is a matter of character, not a matter of keeping a list of rules), is the reason why the word "fruit" is singular. Paul lists nine items. But they all cluster together as a single fruit. Perhaps we should think of them like the segments of an orange, rather than like a bunch of grapes. These nine qualities are not a menu from which you can select a few and ignore the others. They are not like a tick-box exercise where you can tick a few and get a pass mark while failing on the others—as if somebody might say, "Well, I admit that I lose my temper a bit—but hey, I've got plenty of joy!" or, "Okay, I do get a bit rough and sharp with people sometimes, but I'm pretty dependable."

No, the fruit of the Spirit is a single character package. The fruit of the Spirit is not like the gifts of the Spirit, which are distributed among God's people, some to some people, others to other people, all within the body of Christ (1 Cor 12:4-11). The fruit of the Spirit grows all together within a Christian's life, with a unity, wholeness, and balance. All the pieces of the one fruit work together and strengthen each other.

And so, finally, to complete his beautiful statement about the fruit of the Spirit, and as a conclusion to his whole argument in this chapter, Paul gives us a *negative* instruction in verse 24 and a *positive* one in verse 25.

We Are to Say *No* to the Flesh (Gal 5:24)

"Those who belong to Christ Jesus have crucified the flesh with its passions and desires" (Gal 5:24).

This is very strong language. It is also decisive. Paul writes in the past tense—"have crucified." This is not so much an instruction as a statement of reality. Paul is telling us, "This is what you signed up to when you surrendered your life to Jesus. You died! Or rather, you crucified that sinful nature—the flesh."

Now of course Paul did not mean that we no longer have any sinful desires or that we no longer ever actually sin. That kind of sinless perfection is not what the New Testament teaches about our present life. We are sinners saved by grace, but we still live in this world, surrounded by temptation, sometimes falling and failing, but steadily learning and growing. We look forward to being completely freed from sin and temptation only when we live with Christ in the new creation.

Nevertheless, there is an act of will and choice that we are called to exercise day by day. That decisive past fact—you "have crucified the flesh"—has to be translated into a daily present intention. Of course, we must immediately add that this too is a matter of grace and gratitude. It has nothing to do with legalism or earning God's favor by our good behavior. That kind of thinking is utterly contradictory to all Paul teaches us.

Yes, it is all a matter of grace. But, as Paul points out in another place, the grace that *saves* us is also the grace that *teaches* us. Having been saved by grace, we are to live by grace in ways that *exclude* certain kinds of behavior. Here is how Paul makes that double point.

> For the grace of God has appeared that offers salvation to all people. It teaches us to say "No" to ungodliness and worldly passions, and to live self-controlled, upright and godly lives in this present age, while we wait for the blessed hope—the appearing of the glory of our great God and Savior, Jesus Christ, who gave himself for us to redeem us from all wickedness and to purify for himself a people that are his very own, eager to do what is good. (Titus 2:11-14)

Good parents and good teachers know that they have to teach children to be able to say "No" to some harmful and dangerous things. And that is what the loving grace of God does. Once God has *saved* us by grace, God *teaches* us by grace.

So, to make it personal: as a man in Christ, saved by grace and taught by grace, I have to work out what it means to "say 'No' to ungodliness and worldly passions." I have to make it very clear to myself that:

- There are places I should not go.
- There are things I should not look at.
- There are relationships I should not play with.
- There are words I should not allow to pass my lips.
- There are conversations I should not join in or pass on.
- There are feelings I ought to rebuke and suppress.
- There are desires I should not give in to.
- There are attitudes toward others I should not hold . . . and so on.

This does not mean withdrawing from the world into an ascetic, hermit kind of life. Nor does it mean that I sink into a negative, legalistic kind of life in which everything is narrow and restricted by rules. It simply means that I recognize that Christ calls us to a joyful and liberating exercise of self-discipline. For we are in a spiritual battle, and when our sinful human nature sits up and wants to take the steering wheel of our lives, we need to slap it down pretty sharply. Crucify it, says Paul.

But, as John Calvin said in his comment on these verses, "The death of the flesh is the life of the Spirit." So we must move on to Paul's very positive conclusion. He says that we are not to be ruled by law, nor to be ruled by our own sinful nature (the flesh).

We Are to Say *Yes* to the Spirit (Gal 5:25)

"Since we live by the Spirit, let us keep in step with the Spirit" (Gal 5:25).

This sentence is very typical of the way Paul writes. It combines a statement and then a command (or an indicative followed by an imperative, if you like that kind of language). He tells us a truth about ourselves, and then tells us the implication for what we should do as a response.

It is also beautifully balanced with the word "Spirit" like a pivot in the center. His word order in Greek is: "Since we live by the Spirit, by the Spirit let us march."

So he starts with a fact. "We live by the Spirit." That means we are spiritually alive because God has given us new life through his Spirit. It all begins when we are born again through faith in Jesus Christ. At that moment, God takes up residence in our lives through the presence of his Holy Spirit, which is, of course, the presence of the Lord Jesus Christ himself.

Paul has already emphasized this dimension of our Christian experience earlier in the letter. "I have been crucified with Christ and I no longer live, but Christ lives in me. The life I now live in the body, I live by faith in the Son of God, who loved me and gave himself for me" (Gal 2:20).

And the Galatians, who had come to the same experience through Paul's preaching had, as Paul put it, began "by means of the Spirit" (Gal 3:3)—that is, they knew that it was the Spirit of God that had given them new life in Christ and the blessing of belonging to the people of God as children of Abraham.

So then, that being the case, "since we live by the Spirit, let us keep in step with the Spirit" (Gal 5:25). *The New English Bible* captures the balance of fact and instruction, "If the Spirit is the source of our life [that's the fact], let the Spirit also direct our course" [that's the instruction].

Paul uses a vivid metaphor. It is not the ordinary word for walking. It is a word associated with military drills and marching into battle. Soldiers are trained to keep in step with each other, to stay in line, in order to face the enemy with united strength, "shoulder to shoulder," as we might say.

When I was a boy I belonged to one of the many Boys Brigade companies in Belfast (we all thought it was the best one—the 34th Belfast!). I remember the weekly marching drill sessions very well. It was very important to listen to the commands of the officer and follow them instantly without breaking step. Paul is thinking of something like that here. If the Spirit orders an "About Turn," don't go marching straight on. If the Spirit says, "Left Turn," don't swing off to the right. I used to love marching behind our company's silver band, right behind the big base drummer (I envied him!) when we went out on public parade in the streets of Belfast. It was very important for the boys on parade to follow the beat of the band. In other words, if you're following the band, keep in step with the band! Again, that is the kind of image Paul has here. Listen to the music and beat of the Spirit, through the teaching of God's word, and keep in step with him.

Now, we are all aware that sometimes the role of the Holy Spirit in the life of the church can be controversial. Sadly, people fall into division and hostility over what they think of as being "Spirit-led," or how they view the exercise of the gifts of the Spirit in worship and ministry. This is a shame, since we ought to emphasize much more what Paul teaches here, that is, the way the Holy Spirit is at work in our *lives and character*, in being the kind of people who bear the fruit of the Spirit. It is surely very ironic and tragic if those who speak most loudly about the *gifts* of the Spirit are themselves failing to show much of the *fruit* of the Spirit.

The opposite danger is present, too, of course—that we become so afraid of the problems that may be caused by talking about the Spirit that we neglect him altogether. Some people want to emphasize the Word, rather than the Spirit. But that would be to make a false dichotomy, and it would not be faithful to the teaching of the Apostle Paul.

The Lausanne Movement held its Third Congress on World Evangelization in Cape Town in October 2010, and it produced *The Cape Town Commitment: A Confession of Faith and a Call to Action*. I very much like the way it stresses the importance of *both* the Holy Spirit *and* the Word of God in the Christian life in general and in our mission in the world in particular. It is worth quoting some of its paragraphs in full to emphasize this point. Notice how these statements stress the importance of character and behavior, expressed practically in how we live and serve God in our lives—as the work of both the Spirit and the Word of God.

Here, first, is some of what it says about the Holy Spirit:

We love the Holy Spirit within the unity of the Trinity, along with God the Father and God the Son. He is the missionary Spirit sent by the missionary Father and the missionary Son, breathing life and power into God's missionary Church. We love and pray for the presence of the Holy Spirit because without the witness of the Spirit to Christ, our own witness is futile. Without the convicting work of the Spirit, our preaching is in vain. Without the gifts, guidance and power of the Spirit, our mission is mere human effort. And without the fruit of the Spirit, our unattractive lives cannot reflect the beauty of the gospel.

And here is some of what it says about the Word of God. The section titled "We Love God's Word" includes three paragraphs titled "The person the Bible reveals," "The story the Bible tells," and "The truth the Bible teaches." Then it continues as follows:

> *The life the Bible requires.* "The Word is in your mouth and in your heart so that you may obey it." Jesus and James call us to be doers of the Word and not hearers only. The Bible portrays a quality of life that should mark the believer and the community of believers. From Abraham, through Moses, the Psalmists, prophets and wisdom of Israel, and from Jesus and the apostles, we learn that such a biblical lifestyle includes justice, compassion, humility, integrity, truthfulness, sexual chastity, generosity, kindness, self-denial, hospitality, peacemaking, non-retaliation, doing good, forgiveness, joy, contentment and love—all combined in lives of worship, praise and faithfulness to God.
>
> *We confess that we easily claim to love the Bible without loving the life it teaches—the life of costly practical obedience to God through Christ. Yet "nothing commends the gospel more eloquently than a transformed life, and nothing brings it into disrepute so much as personal inconsistency. We are charged to behave in a manner that is worthy of the gospel of Christ and even to 'adorn' it, enhancing its beauty by holy lives." For the sake of the gospel of Christ, therefore, we recommit ourselves to prove our love for God's Word by believing and obeying it. There is no biblical mission without biblical living.*

EPILOGUE

We began this book with the lifetime daily prayer of John Stott. And we end it with some quotations from the last sermon he ever preached, at the Keswick Convention in July 2007. He later included that sermon in his book *The Radical Disciple*. His theme was Christlikeness. He preached passionately that God's supreme will for all Christian believers is that we should become more and more like Christ.

Stott argued we are to be like Christ in his incarnation (Phil 2), in his service as a slave (Jn 13), in his self-giving love (the cross), in his endurance of suffering (1 Pet 2:21), and in his mission (Jn 17:18; 20:21). Then he moved on to the theme of

> ***Christlikeness and the challenge of evangelism.*** Why is it that our evangelistic efforts are often fraught with failure? Several reasons may be given ... but one main reason is that we don't look like the Christ we proclaim. ...
>
> A Hindu professor, identifying one of his students as a Christian, once said, "If you Christians lived like Jesus, India would be at your feet tomorrow."

Finally, Stott came to the question of how we can ever become like Christ, and his answer connects with his daily prayer, and with the whole of this book.

Christlikeness and the indwelling of the Spirit. I have spoken much about Christlikeness, but how is it possible for us? In our own strength it is clearly not, but God has given us his Holy Spirit to enable us to fulfill his purpose. William Temple used to illustrate the point from Shakespeare in this way:

It's no good giving me a play like *Hamlet* or *King Lear*, and telling me to write a play like that. Shakespeare could do it. I can't.

And it's no good showing me a life like the life of Jesus and telling me to live a life like that. Jesus could do it, I can't.

But if the genius of Shakespeare could come and live in me, then I could write plays like his.

And if the Spirit of Jesus could come and live in me, then I could live a life like his.

God's purpose is to make us like Christ, and God's way is to fill us with his Holy Spirit.

Perhaps the best way to finish is with the gentle prayer song written by Albert Orsborn, which combines the longing for Christlikeness with the work of the Spirit.

Let the beauty of Jesus be seen in me
All his wondrous compassion and purity
O thou Spirit divine, all my nature refine
Till the beauty of Jesus be seen in me.

NOTES

Chapter 2: Joy

48   *We love the story: The Cape Town Commitment*, © 2011 The Lausanne Movement, 1.8.B-C.

Chapter 7: Faithfulness

124   *a long obedience:* Eugene H. Peterson, *A Long Obedience in the Same Direction* (Downers Grove, IL: InterVarsity Press, 1980).

Conclusion

160   *We love the Holy Spirit: The Cape Town Commitment*, © 2011 The Lausanne Movement, 1.5.

161   *The life the Bible requires:* Ibid., 1.6.D.

Epilogue

163   *Christlikeness and the challenge:* John R. W. Stott, *The Radical Disciple* (Downers Grove, IL: InterVarsity Press, 2010), 35-36.

164   *Christlikeness and the indwelling:* Ibid., 36-37.

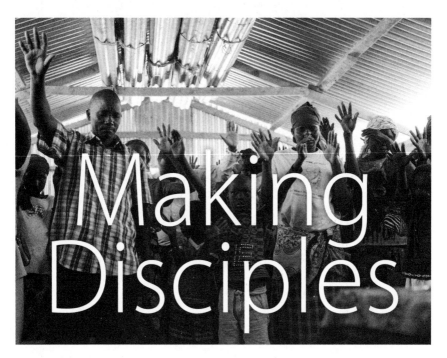

Making
Disciples

Around the World — Christianity is exploding
with growth in numbers

Yet — Believers are struggling to grow in Christ

That's Why Langham Exists

Our Vision
To see churches in the Majority World equipped for mission
and growing to maturity in Christ through the ministry of pastors
and leaders who believe, teach and live by the Word of God.

www.langham.org

FOUNDED BY JOHN STOTT

Langham®
PARTNERSHIP

ALSO BY
CHRISTOPHER J. H. WRIGHT

Knowing God the Father Through the Old Testament
Knowing Jesus Through the Old Testament (Second Edition)
Knowing the Holy Spirit Through the Old Testament

From the Bible Speaks Today Series:
The Message of Ezekiel
The Message of Jeremiah
The Message of Lamentations

The Mission of God: Unlocking the Bible's Grand Narrative
Old Testament Ethics for the People of God
Salvation Belongs to Our God: Christian Doctrine in Global Perspective